THE *Spirituality*
OF GRANDPARENTING

RALPH MILTON

WITH BEVERLEY MILTON

THE *Spirituality* OF GRANDPARENTING

Northstone

Concept: Northstone Team
Editor: Mike Schwartzentruber
Cover and Interior design: Verena Velten and Margaret Kyle
Proofreading: Dianne Greenslade
Photo credits: see page 160

Northstone is an imprint of **Wood Lake Publishing, Inc.** Wood Lake Publishing acknowledges the financial support of the Government of Canada, through the Book Publishing Industry Development Program (BPIDP) for its publishing activities.

BRONZE
BNC CERTIFIED | BIBLIOGRAPHIC DATA 2007-08

At Wood Lake Publishing, we practice what we publish, being guided by a concern for fairness, justice, and equal opportunity in all of our relationships with employees and customers. Wood Lake Publishing is an employee-owned company, committed to caring for the environment and all creation. Wood Lake Publishing recycles, reuses, and encourages readers to do the same. Resources are printed on 100% post-consumer recycled paper and more environmentally friendly groundwood papers (newsprint), whenever possible. A percentage of all profit is donated to charitable organizations.

Library and Archives Canada Cataloguing in Publication
Milton, Ralph
The spirituality of grandparenting / Ralph Milton ; with Beverley Milton.

Includes bibliographical references.
ISBN 978-1-896836-86-7

1. Grandparents – Religious life. 2. Grandparenting – Religious aspects
– Christianity. I. Milton, Beverley, 1937- II. Title.

BV4528.5.M54 2007   248.8'45   C2007-903964-2

Published by Northstone
9590 Jim Bailey Road, Kelowna, BC V4V 1R2 Canada
www.northstone.com
250.766.2778

Printing 10 9 8 7 6 5 4 3 2 1
Printed in Canada

Contents

DEDICATION

This book is dedicated
(of course!)
to our wonderful grandchildren
Zoë Rachel and Jacob Daniel

and to the memory of
their other grandparents
Margaret and Frank McNair
with whom we shared
the joy of their young lives.

ACKNOWLEDGMENTS

This book has been, in many ways, a community effort. Special thanks go to my two best friends – Bev Milton, my wife; and Jim Taylor, my colleague – for their encouragement, love, support, and useful suggestions. And to Kari, Don, Jake and Zoë McNair, who checked the manuscript to make sure I hadn't slandered them too outrageously.

Thanks also to the online community that enriched these pages with their comments and stories.

Thanks also to the staff and Wood Lake Publishing, especially to Lois Huey-Heck for her encouragement to undertake this book in the first place, to Mike Schwartzentruber for his patient and perceptive editing, and to Verena Velten for her inspired layout and graphics.

1

The Grandparent's Vocation

Zoë was three, I think. She was leaning back into her grandma Bev, who had her arms gently wrapped around her grandchild. Zoë's eyes were half closed, as were Bev's. They had that "all-is-well-in-my-world" look. They were rocking and singing. When each song was finished, one of them would start a new one and the other would join in.

I had never really thought of *Mary Had a Little Lamb* or *The Itsy Bitsy Spider* as hymns. They're not included in any hymnbook I know of.

But I realized how profoundly spiritual such songs can be — that their spirituality depends not on the words or the melody, but on who is singing the song. And to whom.

And with whom. And why.

Zoë and her grandmother rocked and sang, quietly, gently, one song after another, some of them several times.

Neither of them were thinking much of anything. They were just being with each other in deep and intimate communion. That's when I realized that *The Itsy Bitsy Spider* can be a hymn. Sacred. Beautiful. Holy.

I can't define or explain or describe God. But if you asked, I would point to the child and the woman singing their togetherness.

You could describe what I saw as a child and a woman simply sitting and rocking and singing. And that would be quite accurate. But if you have eyes and heart to see the holiness, then you see so much more.

Zoë and her Grandma Bev

God may not be an old man with a long white beard, but nothing beats more in harmony with the Divine than a grandparent's heart.

– Basil Pennington

THE CAST OF CHARACTERS

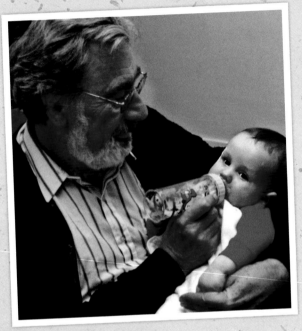

Jake and his Grandpa Ralph

To get you into this book, a few introductions are in order. You've met two of the cast of characters: Bev and Zoë.

Bev and I have been married for half a century. To each other.

Zoë is our granddaughter, the now 11-year-old child of our daughter, Kari, and her husband, Don. Their eldest child is Jake, who is 13.

Like all grandparents, Bev and I are not the slightest bit objective about our grandkids. (Somebody once said that a genius is a slow-learner with grandparents.)

Not as prominent but very much a part of the story is Don's family, the McNair clan. In the beginning, that circle centred on grandparents Margaret and Frank McNair, but they have died, and the extended family continues with four aunts and uncles, and assorted cousins.

Then there's me. Since the words in this book are mine, you need to know about my biases and blind spots so you can take those into consideration as you read.

I am incurably religious. I'm deeply involved in the Christian church because I can't hang on to my spirituality without it. Bev is an ordained minister.

I make no apology.

My Spirituality

Many years ago I attended a lecture on the Jewish faith given by Rabbi Herman Wosk. I asked him about all the traditions and practices of Judaism. (There seemed to be so many.) "Wouldn't it be possible to have the Jewish faith without all that stuff?"

The rabbi picked up the glass of water sitting on the lectern and poured a bit of the water on the floor.

"The water on the floor and the water in the glass – it's all the same water," he said. "But I need it in a glass so I can drink it."

The stories, the songs, the festivals, the teachings, the Bible, even the dumb things the church sometimes does – that's the container, the vessel in which I hold my spirituality. St. Paul called it an "earthen vessel."

Mine is cracked and leaky, but it's *my* vessel. And the people in the church are my tribe. They are my folks. I love them all, and sometimes they make me so mad I could spit.

My religion is like my language. I am writing in English not because it's superior or inferior to any other

Religion can easily become a set of affirmations, stories, and unquestioned metaphors; spirituality recognizes that beyond anything we can express in words, there is always more, an unexpected amazement and awe.

– James Taylor, *Author*

language, but because it's the only one I have. Likewise, my spirituality and the container, the particular Christian tradition, in which I hold it and express it are not superior or inferior to yours or to any others.

But that spirituality is not something I can define. I can circle around it and tell stories about it, but a definition would nail it down and kill it.

A final confession – I am a romantic optimist. I look at the world through rose-coloured bifocals. You'll notice that rosy haze throughout this book.

A GRANDPARENT'S VOCATION

Our spiritual vocation as grandparents is to delight in our grandchildren. That's a one-sentence summary of everything in this book.

It is so easy to write, and so hard to live. It's the living of this spiritual vocation in the real world that takes up the rest of these pages.

To define a word like "grandparent" would be useless. There are so many kinds. So let's glance at a few samples. (I'll get to "spiritual" and "vocation" later.)

Grandparents come in every imaginable shape and size and relationship and circumstance, just like their grandchildren. There are grandparents of adopted children, grandparents living with the pain and tension of a marriage breakup, grandparents of grandchildren in trouble, surrogate grandparents, and grandparents delighting in

(and sometimes hating) a variety of ethnic and religious mixes. Most grandparents today have a long-distance relationship with their grandchildren, whom they see only once in a while.

Because grandparents come in all these varieties and more, there are naturally many styles and kinds of grandparenting. But all of them have two things in common. They are about a relationship between older adults and children. And they meet a mutual need.

Please notice that I didn't say it was a happy relationship. Because it isn't always. Grandparenting can be very painful.

Please also notice that I didn't say grandchildren fill *all* our needs, or that we fill *all* their needs. They can't and we can't and none of us should try.

If you've been thinking of spending your retirement years on a beach or a shuffleboard court, please seriously reconsider. Somehow, and for some reason, you have received the gift of extra years. The way you use this gift is critical to the future of humanity.

- ARTHUR KORNHABER, *AUTHOR*

A vocation is not the same thing as a job or a hobby.

A vocation is something you feel *called* to do. There is something inside you, or something in your spiritual practice that tells you it is important to do this. It's the thing that gets you out of bed in the morning. It's the work that gives your life meaning. You may be paid for that work. Or not. If you find what you are doing fulfilling and meaningful, then it is a vocation.

Many grandparents would call this sentimental nonsense. Everything they do is for fun, or out of habit, or because they need the money, or because they feel the pressures of family and neighbours. Often they do what they do because they feel deeply guilty.

Before we get too judgmental, we should admit that all of us are like that to some degree. We all overdo the "sweetness and light" of grandparenting from time to time. And of course we're not immune to family and social pressures.

But without a vocation, life becomes shallow and unsatisfying. This becomes more and more true as we get older. Seniors without a vocation are more likely to suffer physical and emotional distress in their later years. Reading this book and becoming a spiritual grandparent could help you live more happily, and longer.

SPIRITUALITY

The idea that seniors with a vocation live longer and more happily, is not just a convenient thought I picked out of the air. A number of gerontology studies have demonstrated that people with a lively spirituality tend to live lives that are, in their own estimation, worthwhile and fulfilling. Their spirituality helps them make sense of what's going on – to savour the joys in their life. In the process, they enjoy life even more. Active, lively, and spiritually aware seniors make wonderful grandparents.

Spirituality is a slippery kind of word. I won't try to define it, because that would just get us into some useless semantic arguments.

When you add up all the warm kisses and sticky hands, all the pictures on the refrigerator, the hugs when we come together and the tears when we part, the joys and the disappointments, the religious services and the family arguments – when you add all that together and you

discover that the whole is greater than the sum of the parts, *that's* the spirituality of grandparenting.

In another book in this series, *The Spirituality of Bread*, Donna Sinclair writes,

When the meal is over, our friends gather up leftovers and make sure elderly parents and returning students have generous packages to take with them. This feast, you see, is about more than pie or cake or wine or bread, although all those things are marvellous in their own right.

The spirituality of grandparenting is more than a nice warm feeling. It's more than being able to share your spiritual convictions or religious traditions. It's more than praying for or with your grandchildren. It's all of those things, but more than all of them. It is the fundamental essence that gives grandparenting its meaning.

Spirituality is a shift into a knowing of the heart.

~ SHARON JANIS, *AUTHOR*

Spirituality is the response to the mind-bending questions at the root of it all. Why are we here? What is the point of my life? We can never fully answer those questions, but if the idea of unconditional love is in our minds as we think about these things, we won't be too far off.

Can you have love without spirituality? I doubt it. I know you can't have spirituality without love. Spirituality is living out the love you have for yourself, for your family, and for everyone and everything else in the world.

That's not a new idea. It's been around for thousands of years and it is at the heart of every world religion, though it is expressed in many different ways.

"Gentle character is that which enables the rope of life to stay unbroken in one's hand," goes an African Yaruba proverb.

Khuddaka Patha Buddhism says, "As a mother with her own life guards the life of her own child, let all-embracing thoughts for all that lives be thine."

Islam teaches, "You will not attain piety until you give of what you love; and whatever thing you give, God knows it."

And both Judaism and Christianity teach, "You shall love your neighbour as yourself."

Spirituality is a creative response to questions that can never really be answered. Science can explain much of the "how": how the universe was formed from a big bang many billions of years ago, how plants grow, how babies are formed. But science can have no response to the questions, "Why are we here? What's the point of life?"

When Jake was a toddler, I sat at the kitchen table smiling as Bev invited him to help her make cookies. Logic told me that toddlers are not much help in kitchens, and that Jake was much too young to make cookies anyway. It took Bev longer to make the cookies with Jake's help than it would have taken without him. And there wouldn't have been flour and raisins all over the kitchen floor.

You can be a very good and adequate grandparent without getting this sticky spirituality stuff mixed into it. Except that you'd be missing the best part. You can make perfectly good cookies – maybe better cookies – without a grandchild's help. But the cookies will never taste quite as good.

Look at a rainbow the next time one appears in your sky. Science tells us that it is caused by the refraction of sunlight in droplets of water. An artist tells us that the rainbow is beautiful.

A spiritual person may well be both scientist and artist, but will go beyond both to exclaim, "Wow! To me, that's a symbol of God's love for the world! A symbol of hope!"

Spirituality is about seeing life through a different pair of glasses. It's about the "abundant life" Jesus promised 2,000 years ago. It's the "something more" that Mohammad, the Buddha, Krishna – every world religion – holds out for us.

And that's why I'm standing on this literary soapbox and shouting to anyone who will listen. "Our spiritual vocation as grandparents is to delight in our grandchildren."

But it's kind of messy.

THE PAIN OF GRANDPARENTING

I'm fully aware that grandparenting is not always a walk through the rose garden. Even the best grandparent-grandchild relationship, like every other relationship, has times of pain and fear and anger.

In my research for this book, I had conversations with grandparents who lived with a deep and profound ache because the anger in a marriage break-up meant they had no contact at all with their grandchildren. I spoke with grandparents whose grandchildren were struggling with terrifying diseases, or whose grandchildren had died.

While the huge changes in sexual morality in the last half-century have brought liberation to some, they have brought deep pain and family disagreements to others.

I discovered that the most common longing – a deep ache sometimes – is in grandparents who live far away from their grandchildren. Other grandparents are still working and find it hard to free up enough time and energy for their grandchildren.

All of that struggle and pain is part of this book, but I won't do more than just touch on it. I don't have the training and the skills to analyze or offer advice to those who are struggling with pain and disappointment. I don't ignore that hurt, but I'm not qualified to deal with it.

The recognition of this spiritual dimension of the [grandparenting] relationship explained to me why people experience such deep joy when this "vital connection" is fulfilled, and such profound pain when it is severed.

–Arthur Kornhaber, *AUTHOR*

GRANDPARENTOLOGY

I am, however, superbly qualified to celebrate the spiritual vocation of grandparenting. No, I don't have a degree in spiritual grandparenting. I don't think there is such a thing.

If there was, it would have to be a combination of gerontology, early childhood education, improv theatre, and social work. There would probably be a practicum on humour in there somewhere. And a fair bit of philosophy. In fact, to qualify as a grandparent, we probably should have at least half a dozen years of specialized training.

Fortunately, most grandparents have far better qualifications. Most of us did our undergraduate training as parents. Once we've been a parent, it's hard to stop paying attention to children and to the lessons they can teach us.

LEARNING AND TEACHING TRUST

My first course in "grandparentology" came a couple of years before my own grandkids came along. My teacher's name was Angela. She was six months old at the time.

Angela brought her parents to our house for a visit. After she had been fed, I held her on my knee for a while. Naturally, she burped a bit of dinner onto my shirt. Her mother apologized far more than was necessary, but Angela didn't think a bit of friendly vomit was a problem. She smiled and bubbled and stiffened her legs to stand up on my lap.

And then I realized. Angela trusts me! She does!

She shouldn't of course. I am not a very reliable person. I've let lots of people down and will probably let her down someday. But Angela is only six months old and *has* to trust the adults in her life. She has no choice.

I am a little older than Angela and I have alternatives. I don't trust everyone the way Angela does. I trust

Angela, but then what can she do to me besides spit up on my shirt?

Former U.S. president Lyndon Johnson was quoted as saying he never trusted anyone unless he had that person's career in his pocket. Johnson did not understand "trust." Trust is not the same as mutual fear.

As we get older, we may find we have no alternative but to trust certain people. We will need care just as Angela needs care. We hope we can trust our children, or the caregiver at an institution — trust that they will not take advantage of our vulnerabilities. Can we learn that from our grandchildren?

A large slice of spirituality has to do with trust. It's the kind of trust little people like Angela show in old people like me. It's the kind of trust we hope we can have in our family, friends, and caregivers as we get older and weaker.

Spiritual grandparenting is about learning the art of trust from our grandchildren. But as we learn, we teach, and so spiritual grandparenting is also about mentoring our grandchildren in the precious art of trust.

The kind of trust Angela had in the adults in her life is also a lot like the trust we need to have in God, or Creator, or a higher power, or whatever we call that somebody or something out there and in us, in which we invest our spiritual lives.

SEEING BEAUTY

That spirituality fills a deep need in our souls for someone to see the beauty in us. We're somehow incomplete without it. People of any age need to believe that they are beautiful – if not in other people's eyes, then at least in the eyes of God.

As a wise old lady once said, "God don't make nothin' ugly."

There's a tender story about a grandma who takes her grandson to the park one day. There's a festival of some sort going on, and there's a lady doing face painting on children.

The grandson wants his face painted. But as he sits down on the stool, the lady doing the painting says, "Oh my! You have so many freckles. There's hardly any space on your face to paint anything." The grandma notices that the boy's face clouds and his shoulders droop.

The painting is done, and the grandma takes the boy for a little walk. They sit down on a park bench. "You know," says the grandmother, "I can't think of anything more beautiful than freckles. Can you?"

The boy smiles, looks up at his grandmother, touches her face gently, and says, "Wrinkles."

We find delight in the beauty and happiness of children that makes the heart too big for the body.

~ RALPH WALDO EMERSON

THE PERFECT GRANDFATHER

Bev and I are now doing graduate studies in grandparentology under the professorship of Zoë and Jake and their parents.

More than a dozen years ago, our daughter Kari tracked us down when we were on a camping trip. She bubbled over with the news: "I'm pregnant!" Bev and I walked around for days with a kind of beatific look on our faces. And I fantasized about being the perfect grandparent.

If I'd stopped to think about it, I would have known I wouldn't make it. Because I remember a similar fantasy before each of my children was born. Nobody was going to be more nurturing, more kind, more understanding. I had read Dr. Spock and several articles in the *Reader's Digest* about how to be a good dad, and I just knew I was going to do it all. I had that fantasy again when Bev and I adopted twins, Grace and Lloyd.

My grandparenting fantasy didn't last as long. It took two or three weeks before I settled down and realized, "Ralph, you didn't manage perfection as a father. What makes you think you can manage perfection as a grandfather?"

24

THE FAMILY CLASSROOM

A major "lesson" in this delightful "school" came when Jake was baptized. He went through the whole process with an expression of detached amusement on his face.

I wondered if he knew the process was primarily for the benefit of his parents and grandparents. We baptize our babies because it helps us to sense the wonder of a loving Creator who creates tiny babies.

Jake needed no explanations. He knew. Not "knew" in the sense that he had any consciousness of knowing something like we adults sometimes think we do. But infants tell us with their actions – their body language – whether they feel safe and loved. Jake's actions showed us that in the warmth of his family he experienced the security of the love that surrounds him.

Jake was baptized in water from the Jordan River, which I had brought with me from a study trip to Israel. For me, that water symbolized the rich heritage of struggle and faith of Jake's Judeo-Christian forebears. He was baptized into a church by his uncle (Brian Jackson), surrounded by two parents, four grandparents, numerous relatives, and members of a church. Jake was surrounded by a commonwealth of faith.

"Now that is one lucky child," I thought at the time. And then, "Now that is a child with a problem!"

Jake is both blessed and cursed, because that same doting family and those same kind friends are leading him from his primitive infant wisdom into adult knowledge and adult ignorance. Whether we choose to or not, we are both leading him and misleading him.

Jake is learning his spirituality from us. Lucky kid. Poor kid.

But Jake, like every child, has God on his side. If somehow in our lives we can show him that, he'll be okay.

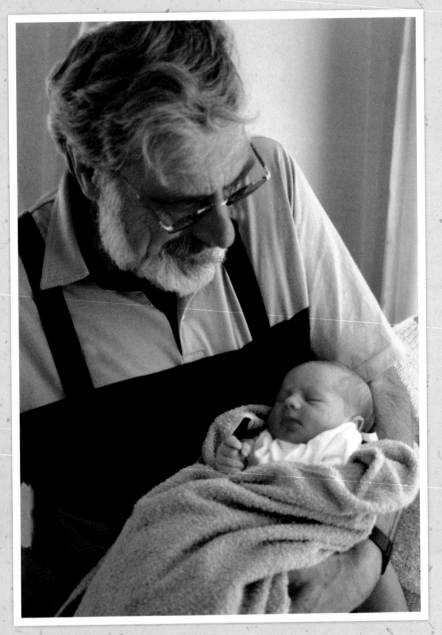

Grandpa Ralph holds a newborn Jake

I learned another lesson in spiritual grandparenting when Zoë Rachel, Jake's sister, was born. She didn't replace her brother as my spiritual teacher. She joined him. And her first lesson to me came three hours after she was born, as I held her in the hospital room, her mom and dad and grandma beaming beside me. Jake stood and looked intently at his brand new sister for about 20 seconds – a long time for a toddler – then decided that the hospital equipment was actually more interesting than this tiny stranger.

Zoë yawned and grimaced and frowned a little. She was thinking! That tiny head, three hours into the world, was thinking!

But how can such a newborn think? What does she know? She has no words. I've not yet seen the colour of her eyes. But something is happening in that tiny mind to cause a grimace and a frown. What kind of consciousness is there in this infant that I already love so much?

The wisdom of a child

Impossible questions? Of course. Our fun-loving God tickles us with such imponderables, and then teases us with other mysteries.

Are we created just to ask such questions? Questions such as, "Why is there pain and awfulness? Why wasn't Zoë born into a world of peace and beauty and tranquility? Why must we all become frail and die?"

Infant Zoë probably was wiser than us all. She simply slept and ate and lived in all the grace that newborns know. Zoë lived in Eden – in the garden of her innocence, where love, not knowledge, was her first reality.

But her brother was already glancing down the pathway to the gate that would take him out of Eden – out of his garden of innocence.

I watched a small scene in that drama not long after Zoë was born. Jake bumped into a floor lamp. Kari asked him to be careful because the lamp might fall. Jake didn't move, so mother picked him up and placed him firmly somewhere else. Jake toddled back to the lamp and touched it, all the while studying his mom to see what she might do. Jake was taking his first necessary toddler steps away from innocence – out of Eden.

I left Eden so very long ago. Innocence is now a faded memory – a vague sense of what I've lost and where I must, someday, return.

LEARNING TO BE A CHILD

The very young and the very old have this in common. They are closest to the heart of their Creator, because newborns have just come from there, and the very old will soon return.

There's an urban legend that reason tells me cannot be factual, but it has truth within it. The mom and dad had brought home a new infant son to meet his older sister now just four years old. She was very attentive to her new brother, but then surprised her parents by asking if she could be in the baby's room alone with him. The parents were a bit hesitant, but they had a baby monitor so they would be able to hear whatever was happening.

So the very young girl went into the room with her infant brother. Over the baby monitor the parents heard her ask, "Tell me about God. I'm starting to forget."

When I hear such stories – when I watch my grandchildren grow – I hear again this ancient wisdom: "Unless you become a child, you cannot return to the heart of your Creator, to that time of peace and joy and hope."

Zoë, Jake! Can you teach me how to be a child again?

Jesus called a child, whom he put among them, and said, "Truly I tell you, unless you change and become like children, you will never enter the kingdom of heaven."

~ MATTHEW 18:2–3, NRSV

A CELEBRATION

The questions buzz and scrape and rattle in my mind, and answers, if there are such things, are no closer now than in my salad days. Why must it be so? Why? And all I hear is silence, or the clatter of new questions loosened by the noise of too much data, too much information.

Perhaps there's nothing that I understand of things that matter. But for one instant, when Zoë Rachel turned her tiny newborn face to me, I knew.

I saw in that infant face a truth that sings my heart to wholeness.

So that's what this book is about. It's a celebration! A party!

It's a way of saying thanks to the world, to our children, to our grandchildren, and to God. A way of saying thanks for being called to delight in our grandchildren. It is a celebration of the spiritual gifts we share and receive between grandparents and grandchildren.

This book is a prayer of thanks to our grandparent God for the wondrous gift of grandchildren.

2

The Many Faces of Grandparents

There is a wonderful cartoon showing a very concerned man beside a very pregnant woman. She is being wheeled into the delivery room. He leans over and says, "Now dear, are you sure you want to go through with this?"

It's a bit like becoming a grandparent. "Do I really want to go through with this? Do I have a choice?" You don't choose whether or not to be a grandparent.

But you *can* choose, at least to some extent, what kind of an experience it will be for you.

Grandparents are not captives of categories.

~ PASCHAL BAUMSTEIN, *AUTHOR*

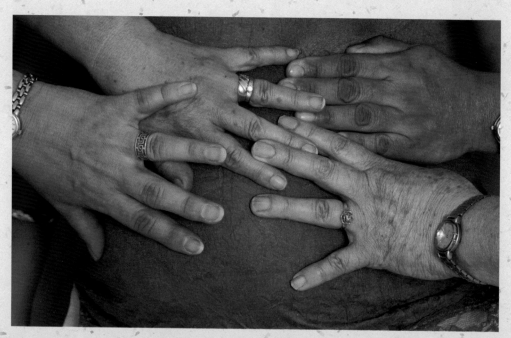

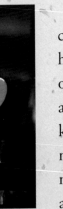

Madeline, a 70-year-old grandmother, wrote the following:

When I was a mom, it was my job to do all the practical things. I had to make sure my kids were dressed for the weather, that they didn't hide their broccoli in their glass of milk. I gave them medicine when they were sick, and hugs when they were hurting.

I'm more philosophical as a grandmother. I have to stand back and observe things from a distance because I know I cannot and must not move in and take my daughter's role as a mother. Remembering my days as a mother, I wish I'd had that opportunity to stand back and watch the bigger picture unfold. But mothers are usually too busy putting on galoshes and going to parent-teacher interviews to be able to do that.

My calling as a grandmother is to watch my grandchildren with wonder, to see them as unique and delightful human beings, each with their own personality and challenges and abilities.

It boils down to this. As a mom, I had to be concerned with the safety and growth of children's bodies. As a grandmom, I am more aware of their happiness and of their souls. And I find it hard not to talk about them.

Madeline's story reminds me of the little girl who went off to Sunday school for the first time. When she got home, her mother asked her how it went.

"It was fun."

"What was your teacher's name?"

"I don't know, but she was Jesus' grandmother."

"Jesus' grandmother?" said the incredulous mom. "Why did you think that?"

"Well, she kept talking about him all the time!"

Jesus' Grandparents

Jesus must have had grandparents, but beyond a name in a genealogy the Bible says nothing about them. In fact, there are very few grandparenting stories in the Bible, but there *is* a wonderful story involving two old and wrinkled seniors, Anna and Simeon.

Mary and Joseph had to do the things required by Jewish tradition. So they brought the baby Jesus to the temple. There they ran into old Simeon, whose face just lit up when he saw that baby. "Now I can die in peace!" he said.

Not that the baby Jesus looked any different from any other baby. But Simeon had a grandfather's insight, and he could see God's promise – God's hope for the future in the face of that perfectly ordinary-looking infant.

Then old Anna came along. Having outlived her husband and most of her children, she spent all her time at the temple. And when she saw that baby she *also* saw that "something" that only old eyes can see – beauty and hope and promise. And the Bible says she went around talking about the child to anyone who would listen.

It is my grandfatherly belief that our spiritual hope can be found in

the face of every new child. People like Anna and Simeon, who have lived long enough to see beyond the obvious, can tell us about it.

AUNTIE FRANCES

Bev and I had four children in our family. When we lived in Teaneck, New Jersey, Bev's parents lived in Victoria, British Columbia, and my mother lived in Winnipeg, Manitoba. Not exactly next door.

Frances was a friend in our church who was a grandmother, but her grandkids lived far away. She needed grandchildren to sit on her lap. Our children needed a grandmotherly lap to sit on.

She would arrive unannounced about once a week, usually with a box of donuts in hand. I would grumble about her ruining the children's appetite just before supper, and she would cheerfully ignore me. Whatever the children were doing, she would join in. They called her "Auntie Frances," but she was being a grandmother to our children.

The relationship filled her needs, and theirs.

Lynn Harden of New York is not a parent herself. She has Jennie, a 19-year-old niece with whom she is very close. Lynn remembers when Jennie was five and she took her swimming. "Jennie didn't know how to swim, but I held her up in the water. She looked up at me with total trust in her eyes," which Lynn felt must be the way we look toward God. "I realized that as a senior adult, I was being God to the child."

MOTHER EMERITUS

After my father died, Mom took a job handling the laundry at the residential School for Deaf Children, in Winnipeg.

Each day when her laundry work was done, she'd go over to the dormitory to spend some time with the deaf children. "Those poor kids living away from their parents really need someone to hold them and love them," Mother said. So she stayed after work almost every day. She played with them, tucked them into bed, kissed their hurts better. At the ripe age of 60, she learned how to sign with her hands. "The children taught me," she said.

When government rules required her to retire at the age of 65, the staff at the school had a nice dinner in her honour. They named her "Mother Emeritus" and gave her a key to the dormitory. So then, because she didn't have to look after the laundry anymore, she had even *more* time for the children.

It wasn't that Mom didn't have grandchildren of her own. But she had lots of "grandmothering" energy left over. She helped fill a need in those children and they helped fill a need in her.

GRANDPARENTS, AS DESCRIBED BY GRANDCHILDREN

My guardian angel is my grandma who died last year. She got a big head start on helping me while she was still down here.

Grandparents are a lady and a man who have no little children of their own. They like other people's.

When they take us for walks, they slow down past things like pretty leaves and caterpillars.

They show us and talk to us about the colour of the flowers and also why we shouldn't step on "cracks."

They don't say, "Hurry up."

They wear glasses and funny underwear.

Grandparents don't have to be smart.

They have to answer questions like "Why isn't God married?" and "How come dogs chase cats?"

When they read to us, they don't skip. They don't mind if we ask for the same story over again.

They know we should have snack-time before bedtime and they say prayers with us every time, and kiss us even when we've acted bad.

My grandmother is a lot like God. They are both old.

A grandmother is a babysitter who watches the kids instead of the television.

Grandmas are moms with lots of frosting.

Usually grandmothers are fat, but not too fat to tie your shoes.

They can take their teeth and gums out.

Grandpas always have time for you when everyone else is too busy.

Everybody should try to have a grandmother, especially if you don't have television, because they are the only grown-ups who like to spend time with us.

An Ethiopian beauty

Grandparenting stories are not always about joy and fulfillment. Almost always, the joy comes mixed with uncertainty, doubt, and sometimes pain.

My closest friend is Jim Taylor – a colleague of many years. When I would talk about my grandchildren, Jim would get a wistful, longing, pained look in his eyes. Jim and his wife, Joan, had two children. Stephen, the eldest, died of cystic fibrosis when he was in his early 20s.

Sharon, their daughter, had never quite found the right partner, someone she wanted to share her life with. But she wanted very badly to be a mother. So she decided to adopt a child, and Jim and Joan found themselves being grandparents to a beautiful baby girl from Ethiopia.

I was delighted, because now when Jim and I have lunch together we can *both* brag about our grandchildren and show each other their pictures.

No cowboy was ever faster on the draw than a grandparent pulling a baby picture out of a wallet.

– SOURCE UNKNOWN

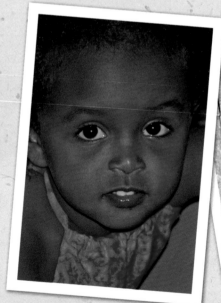

Jim and Joan's Granddaughter Katherine

But Jim tells me there's a tiny though painful worry at the back of his mind.

I hope, I trust, I believe that Katherine will survive the adjustments that confront all adopted children. So much will depend on the friends she chooses, as she grows toward adulthood.

And there I discover a streak of prejudice within myself that I hadn't known I had. Because when I picture her in a cluster of kids, they are black, like her. And I realize that in that context I would be the outsider. Although I know many black people I'd be proud to call my friends, I wince because a shadowy corner of my mind still harbours a few unflattering stereotypes of rebellious black youths, school dropouts, gang members…

I don't want Katherine to hang out with that kind of person. I want her to associate with – well, with educated, intelligent, purposeful kids. Whom I tend to see as white. Like me.

I hope – dear God, how I hope! – that as she grows, as she tests her limits, that I never never never yield to the temptation to blame her genetic legacy. If she were descended from my own DNA, I couldn't. But she isn't. Somehow, I have to wipe that awareness out of my mind, to see only a delightful girl whom I love with all my heart.

But I will never know if I can, until it happens. That's what worries me, about me.

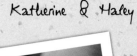

Katherine & Haley

Chuck and Gayda describe themselves as "pretty straitlaced," so when their son, an only child, came home from university and announced that he was gay, Chuck recalls, "he just sent us reeling."

It took me quite a long time to come to this, but I finally decided that I needed my son more than I needed my attitudes about homosexuality.

But that wasn't the end of it. Then he said he was getting married. I was just getting used to that idea when he phoned and said, "You are going to be a grandfather. We are adopting a baby girl."

It was anything but easy. I grew up in the '40s when we didn't even talk about things like that. So Gayda and I were really up against it. We had a choice. Change our attitudes or lose our son. We did some reading. We did some praying, too, which wasn't something we did normally or easily.

There's a happy ending to our story. We have fallen in love with our granddaughter, and we love both her parents. We have a wonderful time together and it all feels so totally normal.

And you know, they say little Cynthia looks a lot like her granddad.

Judith's story

At first, Judith didn't want to tell me her story. "It hurts too much. I can't find the words." But then she sent me an e-mail.

My first reaction to the news of each pregnancy has been, "Oh please, God, no!"

Each time I have struggled to believe that my daughters, who couldn't really take care of themselves, would somehow be able to care for the baby. Or at least give the child up for adoption.

Each time I have struggled with how much to get involved, afraid for my grandchild, afraid for my daughter, and as my health failed, afraid for myself.

My grandchildren have taught me that you can, in fact, die from a broken heart. They were snatched from me by their drug-addicted parents and the stress caused my heart to fail.

I have learned that when I have lost faith and given up hope, my grandchildren remain tethered to me with some kind of string by which, with the strength of desperation, I can pull them back to me.

I learned that love is, above all, an act of will.

Mavis Enns wept bitter tears when she brought her grandchildren home to live with her. "I was crying because they had lost their parents to drugs and alcohol."

According to the U.S. Census Bureau, in 1970, 2.2 million American children lived in a household maintained by a grandparent. By 2005, this number had risen to 4.1 million.

Grandparents of every racial, ethnic, and social background find themselves becoming parents again. Sometimes they have to fight the bureaucracy because grandparents usually have no legal standing when it comes to the care of their grandchildren.

When grandparents take on the role of child rearing, they are parenting, not grandparenting.

It's not within the scope of this book to deal with the joys and sorrows of that situation. But there are some resources named on page 158.

RELIGIOUS DIFFERENCES

During an Elderhostel in Arizona, I talked with a Jewish grandmother who told me of her experience when her daughter married the son of a Baptist minister.

At first I was devastated. I was sure my daughter would convert and my grandchildren would know nothing of their Jewish heritage. But it was more important to me to keep the communication lines open with our daughter.

The funny thing was, the experience made me far more conscious, far more aware of my Jewish traditions – of my Jewish faith. My husband and I had not been particularly observant. We didn't eat pork, but that was about the only dietary rule we kept. We went to synagogue very occasionally.

But when my daughter married a Christian it became more important to me. At first my daughter thought I was doing this as a sneaky way of converting her husband. But that wasn't it. The good thing was we kept talking about it until we really understood each other.

Now I have a wonderful grandchild, who has a nice Jewish nose like my husband. I can be my real self, and I am delighting in my discovery of my rich heritage.

I tell my grandson Bible stories. We light Shabbat candles. My grandson and his parents go to synagogue with me on special days. I give Hanukkah gifts rather than Christmas presents.

I know the boundaries. And we talk about those boundaries. But I don't walk on eggshells. I can be myself and that's wonderful.

I found this grandmother's testimony most interesting, because a few weeks earlier I heard a similar story told by the minister of a conservative Christian church. He spoke of how his horizons had been broadened – how he had come to a new appreciation of his own faith – as he dealt with the reality of his son marrying a Jewish woman and converting to the Jewish faith.

Both of these grandparents agreed that it was far better for their grandchildren to be raised in a faith-filled home than in a home where differences in religious background resulted in no spiritual practice at all.

We will not hide [these stories] from the children… so that the next generation might know them, the children yet unborn, and rise up and tell them to their children.

–PSALM 78, SELECTED VERSES, NRSV

A LONELY FAITH

Husan Kwok is Buddhist. His daughter Su married a Christian and chose to convert. Su and her husband had a lovely son. For a few years they were active church members. Then the husband left. No one is really sure why. Husan tells the story.

Su is trying very hard to raise little Isaac to be spiritually healthy. But they are no longer active in a church community – and there are a lot of reasons for that. Rarely a day goes by when Su doesn't think about changing that void in their lives. They just don't feel at home anywhere.

My daughter took her conversion to Christianity very seriously, more seriously than her husband. She tells me her husband and family are "cultural Christians" who do things like Christmas and Easter and even go to church occasionally, but it makes no difference in their lives.

Su has a deep relationship with God. But she's rather lonely in her faith. She tells me she just doesn't feel at home anywhere.

I'm not trying to convert her back to Buddhism. We do talk together about our faith and our traditions. But we speak different religious languages now, and sometimes I feel there is such a chasm between us.

ADOPTIVE GRANDPARENTS

I remember how pleased I was when my mother came to visit us the day after Bev and I brought home the twins we had adopted. She just slid into the grandmothering role as if she had known Grace and Lloyd since the day they were born. She related to them in the same warm grandmotherly way as she did with Mark and Kari, our birth children.

I also remember feeling a jolt of anger when a friend talked about Grace and Lloyd's "real parents," meaning their birth parents.

"*We* are their real parents," I snapped. "The relationship of love is stronger, more powerful, and far more real than any biological relationship."

Grandparents have a special vocation as the storyteller for their adopted grandchildren. We can talk about the yearning in the heart of the child's parents for someone "just like you." We can tell them about the delight and fulfillment we experienced when we first met them.

"Some babies grow in their mother's tummy," we can tell them. "But you grew in your mom's heart."

Yes, of course you should romanticize the story a little bit. And don't leave out the part about how a loving Creator drew you together as a family – about how God wants everyone to have someone to love.

Susan, Blake, and Tién, who are a part of our extended McNair family, celebrate "family day" every year – "the day we became a family." In Tién's personal storybook it says, "When I was a little baby, my mom and dad came to Vietnam and we got adopted, to love each other forever."

WINDS OF GRIEF

Annabelle Green of Montreal lost her only grandchild when he was five years old.

But I still feel like a grandparent. I treasure those memories. And so I always tell grandparents, "Use your religion – your faith tradition – whatever you want to call it. Because you are going to need it!" Parents and grandparents who don't use the rich traditions of their faith leave themselves vulnerable.

I have this picture in my mind, how the priest held him up, like a chalice toward the altar, which connected my grandson to the heart of God. I don't believe for a moment that he needed baptism to keep him from going to hell or anything like that. I mean, that's ridiculous.

Annabelle says the sense that her grandson is now part of God comforts her when she struggles with the "fierce winds in the canyon of my grief."

Shared grandchildren

Bev and I have two grandchildren, Zoë and Jake. Ours has been a very traditional grandparent relationship. Our daughter, Kari, married Don, the son of Frank and Margaret McNair, who were friends of ours and active in our church. They lived just a few blocks from our house.

Frank and Margaret and Bev and I would get together often. Sometimes we'd go travelling together, and it was great fun sharing stories about our grandchildren because we were talking about the same kids. And I would stoutly maintain that all of Zoë and Jake's best characteristics were inherited from me. Of course the other three claimed the same thing.

Our grandchildren came along just about the time Bev and I were retiring. Bev had to leave her work as a minister because of her health. That left a big, aching hole in her life. "God sent me grandchildren just when I needed them," she said.

GRANDPARENTING IS NOT FOR SISSIES

I read a book once called *Old Age Is Not for Sissies*. Which is true. You wake up in the morning and you are grateful that everything seems to hurt, because you know that "if it ain't hurtin' it ain't workin'."

Grandparenting is not for the faint of heart either. And old age and grandparenting have a habit of coming about the same time. Grandparenting takes courage, imagination, and patience. And strength. Not often the physical kind, but emotional and spiritual strength.

The grey-haired grandma and grandpa, she with her knitting and he whittling a block of wood, sitting before the fire surrounded by their lovely, adoring grandchildren – that scene doesn't exist except on a few greeting cards.

Grandparenting is a calling. A demanding though delightful calling. A spiritual vocation. It's the best way to spend the last third of your life.

But it is not easy!

3

The Long Adventure Called Life

I have finally figured out why time seems to pass so much more quickly the older we get.

Zoë's birthday is in mid-December and mine is near the end of that month. So sometimes we celebrate together. When Zoë was three and I was 65, her cake had three candles and mine a single candle. "We didn't want to set off the smoke alarm," said daughter Kari.

Then it struck me. For Zoë, a year was a third of her life. For me, a year was 1/65 of my life. As each year goes by, it represents a smaller proportion of our entire life. And so time speeds up for us grandparents. (Albert Einstein's famous theory says something about time being relative, but he probably wasn't thinking of birthdays.)

Grandchildren are God's way of compensating us for growing old.

– Mary H. Waldrin

Even now, when Zoë is knocking on the teenage door, I'm sure she can't imagine what she will be like – what her life will be like – when she is 65. But Bev and I are a part of her life now, and we are showing her a couple of models of what an old person might be like.

That's why there's a fair bit in this chapter about aging. Aging and grandparenting go hand in hand. Spirituality is a big part of both those realities.

We do our best learning when we are young. Zoë and Jake are fortunate, because they have had four grandparents to learn from. Four models of aging.

Not perfect models. Not even good models sometimes. But the canvas of their future is not blank. They have some sense of what "old" is like, and bad examples can be almost as useful as good examples.

Becoming a grandmother is wonderful. One moment you're just a mother. The next you are all-wise and prehistoric.

~ Pam Brown

A THREE-WHEELED PHILOSOPHER

Bev and I were staying at Redeemer College in Hamilton, Ontario, a number of years ago. It was a beautiful day and I was sitting on a chair out on the lawn, reading. I had just decided to retire from my work as a publisher, but the decision raised a batch of unnamed anxieties.

Along the sidewalk came a girl on a tricycle – about six years old was my guess. We smiled at each other. Then she stopped, gave me a most intense look, and asked, "Are you old?"

I'm usually quite quick off the lip, but the child's question stopped me cold. She waited. Maybe she knew she had asked a profoundly disturbing question. Eventually, I responded, "Yes. Yes, I am."

Then she said, "Will you play with me?"

Were the two questions connected in her mind? They were in mine. They said to me, "If you are old, I will trust you." For her, none of the bad jokes they throw at people on their birthdays, just, "Will you play with me?" And I wanted so much to do just that, to hear more from this three-wheeled philosopher, to learn from her wisdom and to delight in the joy of her life.

But we lived in a real world, my little friend and I. So I had to say, "I would really like to play with you, but first you need to go and talk to your mom or your dad, and if one of them comes here and tells me it's okay, then we can play."

"My dad doesn't live with me anymore," she said very soberly. "I'll ask my mom."

She didn't return. But she had left her gift with me. She had changed me from a man, fearful of retirement, angry at his age with its limitations and necessities, to a man delighting in his age and its possibilities – transfigured by the candid, open, affirming trust of a child.

"Yes, I would really like to come and play with you."

Appreciating wrinkles

I love being an old man. I am brow enhanced (politically correct for going bald) and distinguished (i.e., mostly grey), and I am wondering if all my hair will turn white before it all falls out. I'm taking bets. The odds are 2 to 1 that the baldness wins.

I sometimes get a bit ticked off by well-meaning young people who offer advice and help based on their own needs and priorities. It's a very different experience being old, and we find ourselves with very different needs. Unfortunately, we seniors aren't very good at explaining what it's like.

Old is not a disease. Old is an accomplishment. It took me the traditional three score years and ten to develop all my wrinkles.

I really appreciated my wrinkles after a little experiment I did. I took a photo of my face, with all its 70-plus years of wrinkles, and scanned it into my computer. Then I used a software program called Photoshop to remove all the wrinkles. There I was, with a face as smooth as a baby's bottom.

I looked ghoulish! Ghastly!

I didn't look young. I looked as if I'd been embalmed! Baptized in Botox!

So I will keep every one of my wrinkles, thank you very much! I earned them. The wrinkles tell you where the smiles and tears have been.

I enjoy my wrinkles and regard them as badges of distinction – I worked hard for them!

– Maggie Kuhn, *author and founder of The Gray Panthers*

I am deeply grateful to my son-in-law, Don, for the gift of memories he gave my grandchildren. For most of a decade, Don loaded the kids into the car and took them the hour's drive to visit his parents.

During that time Frank, Don's father, wrestled with failing eyesight and Parkinson's disease. He eventually chose palliative care and his death followed soon after.

Margaret, Don's mother, moved into a senior's residence, and there she wrestled with fading memory until she too passed away.

I asked Don why he worked so hard to make sure his children spent time with their grandparents, because it certainly wasn't always

Jake with Frank,
his other grandpa

convenient and he is a busy professional and always pushed for time.

I did it because of the fine memories I have of visiting my own grandparents. It was always a warm and safe place to be. At their summer cottage or when they came to our house. I played soldier with my grandmother's spoons, and with the collection of spools she saved from her sewing. Their house had a musty smell, so that even now I find mustiness a pleasant smell. To this day I think of my grandparents on my mother's side when I smell roast beef, or when I smell cigars.

In his final years, Frank found it hard to converse. By this time he was almost totally blind, and Parkinson's disease had taken his voice away. But his hearing was fine. As Don said,

Even though Dad couldn't converse with the kids, it was clear he listened intently to everything that was going on.

My mother's dementia often had her feeling really confused and angry and fearful. But she seemed to thrive on children. When the room was full of noisy kids, she'd perk right up and you could see she was really enjoying things.

I asked Zoë and Jake what they remembered most about their grandpa Frank and grandma Margaret. "I liked to go see Grandma because she liked my friends," said Jake. "I remember hugging Grandpa goodnight because he would go to bed before we left to go home. I remember how they used to tell Grandpa what was on his plate because he couldn't see it. 'The carrots are at two o'clock, and the meat is at six o'clock.'"

Zoë said she liked bringing her friends to Grandma's "because we would eat in the dining room which was like a restaurant. My friend Emma liked to come with me because she'd get to eat meat. Her parents are vegetarian. And Grandma liked it when we showed her things we had made or brought from school."

Our grandchildren accept us for ourselves, without rebuke or effort to change us, as no one in our entire lives has ever done, not our parents, siblings, spouses, friends — and hardly ever our own grown children.

– RUTH GOODE, *AUTHOR*

I asked Kari how Zoë and Jake had responded to the death of their grandparents. "They were prepared," she said. "It didn't come as a surprise or a shock to them. In both cases, they were aware that their grandparents were fading, and close to the end. They knew death was imminent. So there was sadness, of course, but not shock or surprise."

Don spoke with intensity about the priceless gift his parents gave his children.

The legacy my parents left for my children is this. You are never too old to be loved. You are never too sick to be loved. You may be forgetful and strange, you may be old and frail, but the love is still there.

When we gathered at the graveside to bury the ashes, first the ashes of my father and then years later of my mother, I hoped the children would sense that they are part of an extended family. That extended family is not just there for fun or playing games with their cousins – that too, but the sense that this family is part of you, and you are a member of the clan.

A financial planner offered us a package of insurance in case either Kari or I would be incapacitated and unable to function. We didn't need it. When you have an extended family, that is your insurance. The sad thing is that so many families need that insurance because they have nothing else to fall back on.

SUCCESSFUL AGING

When Bev and I got ready to retire, we read assorted books and magazine articles on the subject. They all talked about health and housing and finances. There wasn't even a paragraph titled, "How to grow old."

The reason is obvious. We deny age. There is so much in our culture that tries to help us "stay young." Which is a bit silly when you think of it, because every one of us has a birthday every 365 days, whether we like it or not.

To age or not to age is not an option. Our only choice is *how* to age. Will we go kicking and screaming and hating every sagging muscle and greying hair? Or will we enjoy the changing landscape of life, savouring the opportunities and blessings of age, even as we struggle with the necessary pain and increasing disability?

Frank and Margaret offered our grandchildren an invaluable lesson on aging. Bev and I are continuing that education. It could be the most practical part of their education, because our grandchildren will probably spend more of their lives being old than you or I or our children.

It's in the Details

Did my grandmother have any idea that I was taking note of her every move, stowing away life lessons, every time I came to her house?

— Muriel Duncan, *journalist*

I have a head full of theories and theologies and philosophies. None of that means a thing to my grandchildren. Somehow I need to translate all that theoretical stuff into choosing the kind of detergent I use to wash the dishes, picking my dirty clothes off the floor, shopping for a new pair of shoes, and deciding what kind of food to buy and eat.

"Don't sweat the details," someone once said to me, but it is precisely in the details that we live our spirituality. It's in the tiny acts of kindness or cruelty to family, friends, and colleagues – so tiny they mostly go unnoticed – that our faith is (or is not) expressed.

It's the details that grandchildren pick up on. Especially when they are very young. The way we treat the person at the grocery checkout, the way we talk about the neighbours, the way we treat each other in the family.

I've heard people tell their children, "Don't do as I do. Do as I say." But it doesn't work. We probably should have learned that in raising our own children who turned out to be more like us than we really wanted – especially once they moved from being teenagers into adulthood.

Well, we have a second chance with our grandchildren. We have a chance to be what we really believe – to live our spiritual convictions.

REMEMBERING THE TEENAGE YEARS

Grandparents see the world through their older eyes and experience events in the context of their longer lives. Sometimes we forget that, whether we like it or not, times have changed.

Here we can go to our grandchildren for help. If we can get them to explain their lives, their schools, their friends, their clothing, their customs – if we can listen to them without preaching little sermons about how things *ought* to be, we will be in a much better position to really understand today's world. Only then can we offer intelligent and relevant comments from our longer life experience.

For me, it helps to remember how my parents hated the clothes I wore and the music I liked. When I look at my old high school graduation photos, I remember how scandalized my dad was at the pants that were cut extravagantly wide at the knees, with tiny little cuffs, and three French seams down the side. I had a suit jacket with exaggerated shoulder pads, so I looked like a walking triangle. We called it a "zoot suit."

My folks hated Johnny Rae, and Rosemary Clooney, and Nat King Cole. Elvis Presley was "demonic" and Louis Armstrong's singing was beyond comprehension. Their intense dislike not only drove a wedge into our relationship, but I dug in my heels and listened to that music as an act of teenage rebellion.

Perhaps one has to be very old before one learns how to be amused rather than shocked.

– PEARL S. BUCK

Today I have some CDs of the music I loved back then. I still enjoy it. Some of it was good and wears well. But some of it, especially the lyrics, was pretty stupid. "Be-bop a lu-la, she's my baby…" isn't exactly great poetry.

Remembering that generation gap, I try to listen with as much of an open mind as I can when my grandchildren talk about their lives. I don't have to like it all, and I don't. But I should try to understand as much of it as possible before I offer my comments.

Recently, Jake let me read an essay he had done in school about Goth culture. I'd never even heard of Goth culture before. It's a kind of anti-everything culture of teens and young adults who are into wild, multicoloured hair, body piercing, tattoos – anything to get a reaction from old folks like me.

My first response could easily have been to condemn this sort of thing and to tell Jake how ugly and stupid the whole thing is. That would have pushed him toward embracing this kind of culture, and more importantly, driven a wedge between the two of us. Instead, we looked at the pictures he had gathered and laughed at the outrageousness of it all. And I wrote a humorous little postscript, which he attached when he handed in the essay at school.

An hour with your grandchildren can make you feel young again.
Anything longer than that and you start to age quickly.

~ GENE PERRET, *HUMOURIST*

When our grandchildren are teenagers, we older folk have to work really hard on our own attitudes and responses. I'm not for a moment suggesting that we should give up our values, our standards, our morality, our spirituality, and accept everything that comes along in youth culture. But if we lose the relationship – if we can no longer converse easily with our grandchildren – then it really won't matter what we believe. They won't hear it.

We have a lot of life and a lot of learning to share with our grandchildren. The hardest part is keeping the lines of communication open. It means we do far more listening and far less preaching.

Grandfathering

Grandfathering didn't come as naturally to me as grandmothering did to Bev. Bev had known two grandmothers, but both my grandfathers were dead long before I was born.

"Grandfathering" is often hard. I think this is because in our own families fathers were the breadwinners. They worked long hours and were not much involved in the nurture of their children. Of course there were lots of exceptions, and I am grateful that my father was one of them.

Nevertheless, when Bev and I married half a century ago, our roles were quite clear. Her job was to populate the world. Mine was to conquer it. We never managed either.

Fortunately for me, the feminist movement came along when we were in the middle of our child-rearing days, and forever changed that concept. Probably not soon enough for our own children, but hopefully I've been able to find the nurturing

spirit in my own soul so that I can now be more of a grandfather to my grandchildren.

When we age into our 50s and 60s, there's a new kind of generativity that percolates in our souls. It's similar to the generativity we sense when we are young men, which leads us into relationships and family life.

When that creative urge comes back in later life, it can find expression in destructive or inappropriate ways, but is best experienced in the relationship with grandchildren. Something new and strong and good stirs in our hearts when we hold a new grandchild. If we listen to our hearts, we can sense a new creativity, a new sense of fulfillment, a new and closer relationship with our Creator.

Still, it's not an easy thing for many men. That's sad. For them and for their grandchildren.

As an aging grandfather I have found my spirit quickened and my faith nurtured by the affection, the enthusiasm, and the essential goodness of my grandchildren. Every day they teach me about the eternal verities of God's universe.

– GEORGE MCGOVERN, *STATESMAN*

There is a solution, but it takes courage and patience. Simply admit, first to yourself and then to your spouse and your children, that you feel like a baboon in a beauty parlour when it comes to children. (Remember: real men don't run away from tough challenges and you are man enough to do what it takes to find the nurturing grandfather inside yourself.)

"So, Hazel. Teach me how to change a diaper?" Watch how others hold a baby and then practise. Laugh at yourself. "Hey! This little guy just pooped all over my clean shirt!"

Most of all, learn to play with your grandchildren. Let yourself be a child and enter into their child's play. I like to wear suspenders rather than a belt (far more comfortable) and so I taught my grandbabies how to pull those elastic suspenders and let them snap back onto my belly. Then I would overreact with great grandfatherly noises.

Speaking of noises, there's a great grandfatherly game you can play when your grandchild is just beginning to learn how to talk. Make noises with your mouth and try to get your grandchild to imitate you. It's not only fun, it's good pre-talking exercise for your grandchild. And it's a good way to purge the stuffy-old-man-in-a-suit personality out of your psyche.

Most of all, remember that grandfathers have a big part to play in teaching grandchildren what a man is really like. This is especially important with grandsons, and critically important if they are living in a one-parent family without regular exposure to a constructive male model.

Think about the kind of man you are and decide if that's the kind of man you want your grandson to imitate. What you *tell* your grandson about being a man doesn't matter a hoot. It is the kind of man you actually *are* that he will store in his brain and that will inform at least a small part of the man he becomes.

And the kind of grandfather he will be when it's his turn.

Minister Emeritus

Bev is the Minister Emeritus at our church. It's a great honour that she really deserves because of all the fine work she has done in her years of ministry.

But she has another qualification for her status as Minister Emeritus. She is a grandmother.

As Minister Emeritus, she has no duties. No job description. She doesn't have to go to any meetings.

It's much the same as a grandparent. She doesn't have to buy clothes for the children or take them to the doctor or go to parent-teacher interviews.

As a Minister Emeritus, Bev tries to attend various events and functions. She's there to applaud or laugh or cry. And she's there to appreciate, one to one, what people have done. She's there to listen when someone just needs a kindly soul to talk to. But she's not a problem solver or a counsellor.

As grandparents, she and I try to attend the school concerts, the ballet recitals, the band concerts, the Christmas pageants. We go to let Jake and Zoë know that what they are doing is important and that we are rooting for them.

When they were very young, we celebrated their first tooth, their first words, their first steps. Then we marvelled at their first piece of art to grace our refrigerator. Today we review each report card with suitable gravity.

Each spring, Zoë's ballet class has a recital. At the end of the performance, when Zoë comes out from backstage, all glittery and smiling, I bow deeply and present her with a small bouquet of roses. She takes my hand, curtsies in the classic style of the ballet, and gives me a very proper little peck on the cheek.

It's a little game, of course. She's my prima ballerina and I'm her admiring suitor. It's a perfect game for a granddaughter and her grandfather. Soon enough there will be other suitors, and I will step aside.

Keeping our feet on the ground

Grandchildren help grandparents keep their feet on the ground. They help us keep in touch with reality when wonderful things happen, and when tragedy hits.

We were with Don and Kari and the two children when word came that our son Lloyd had taken his own life. The fetal alcohol syndrome he received from his birth mother made it impossible for him to recognize and receive love, which eventually led him to his terrible decision.

We sat there, stunned, crying, trying to make sense out of the grief and frustration we felt. Jake was a toddler at the time, with only a few words in his vocabulary. He walked around the room looking at us, no doubt sensing the pain we felt, and obviously concerned by it all.

Then he went to the window, pointed to a vehicle going by, and announced in a loud, clear voice, "Truck!"

Jake seemed to cut right through the grief and the pain. He seemed to be telling us that, yes, the pain was real and terrible, but the world is still turning and life goes on and if you doubt that, take a look through the window. There is a truck going by.

Of course he didn't consciously think those thoughts. But on the other hand, maybe Jake – in his own childlike way – sensed what was going on and wanted to bring us back from the chasm of grief.

A GOLD STAR

A year or so later, Jake brought me back to reality in another way. Again, we were at Don and Kari's house when Clarke Saunders phoned on behalf of St. Stephen's College in Edmonton, and said, "We'd like to know if you would accept an honorary Doctor of Sacred Letters degree."

Would I accept?

When I came down off the ceiling, my son-in-law tried to explain to Jake what Grandpa was so excited about.

You need to know that Jake is a very bright young lad, but he was having a bit of trouble with toilet training. He understood the principle perfectly well, but the diaper system worked fine for him and he could see no reason to change. So his mom and dad devised all sorts of incentives.

Don took a couple of runs at explaining an honorary doctorate to Jake, but he was just not getting through. After several more tries, Jake got the idea. "Oh, it's like when you get a gold star for going pooh in the toilet!"

Jake was absolutely right!

It's all relative. Going pooh in the toilet was as much of an achievement for Jake as getting an honorary doctorate was for me. In pointing that out, Jake helped me, his hyper granddad, get his feet back on the ground.

One mother of a preschool age daughter… heard that you should tell children that boys have a penis and girls have a vulva.

So she taught her daughter that she had a vulva. Like all three-year-olds, the daughter was keen to share the news.

Not long after, Grandmother arrived from Montreal for Christmas.

An hour after Granny's arrival, the little girl asked, "Granny, do you have a vulva?" "No, dear," said Granny, "I have a Toyota."

- Meg Hickling, AUTHOR

Not too long ago, my friend Jim and I were bemoaning the fact that we tend to fall asleep when reading. Or watching TV. Or listening to a speech or sermon. And then we got on to the reality that the head is not the only organ that refuses to remain upright when you most want it to.

I have a young doctor who insists on outrageous prescriptions for what ails me. Like exercise. I prefer to get my exercise jumping to conclusions. He wants me to spend half an hour a day on that mind-numbing devil's invention, the stationary bike. Then he adds cheerfully, "Sex is good exercise, too!" This, after he's just written a prescription for a medication that effectively takes the stuffing out of the old sock.

Every month, Bev and I get a magazine called *Good Times*, which is full of ads for electric wheelchairs and adult diapers. There always seems to be at least one article about what to eat to stay healthy. That's fine, although I'm beginning to think that "health food" is an oxymoron.

What annoys me are the articles so obviously written by young 30- to 50-year-olds who have no idea what it's like to be old. This is especially true when the article is about sex.

They keep trumpeting the idea that even though you're "old and grey and full of sleep and nodding by the fireside," you can still compete in the sexual Olympics. The Special Olympics, mind you. But you can still do it and there is a whole armamentarium of pills and potions to help you succeed.

Hidden between the lines is the subtle (and sometimes blatant) suggestion that unless you are sexually active, you might as well be dead. There's the assumption that we seniors find ourselves absolutely devastated when we're not as randy as the younger royals.

Big news for everyone under 60! Coital sex is not the main show! It's nice when it happens, but it's way down on the priority list. At the top of that list are things like intimacy, tenderness, closeness.

Reclaiming your virginity, I sometimes call it.

It's not usually the grandparent's job to tell their grandchildren about the "birds and the bees." That's the parent's job. Still, as sex educator Meg Hickling points out in her book *The New Speaking of Sex*, more and more grandparents provide after-school care for their grandchildren.

Who gets the child's questions after school? Grandma or Grandpa often feel honoured that they are hearing the questions, but, like parents, they are hesitant about what or how much to say... I encourage them to answer the questions, to educate themselves and those parents [who may not give children an answer], and to demonstrate enthusiasm and joy about healthy attitudes throughout the whole extended family.

Meg's last point is especially important. Our task is to communicate, by the way we act and speak, what a healthy sexuality might be like.

Sexuality as a gift, but not as an obsession.

Sexuality is a spiritual gift through which we can communicate our deep and profound love for another person. Like all great gifts, it can also easily be abused, and then it becomes dangerous.

Shakespeare talked about "second childishness." That happens for some and it's sad. But what's really great is "second child*like*ness."

For me, one of the delights of grandparenting was to have Jake or Zoë climb on my lap. I say "was" because now they're big enough that climbing onto our laps might do serious damage. So they snuggle in beside us. Same thing.

They don't think about it, of course, but at an unconscious level they know they need that closeness and that tenderness with us, and with their parents.

And believe me, Grandpa and Grandma need it as much as they do. Just as I need those many moments of closeness with Bev throughout the day and at night in bed.

Of course that's a form of sexuality. Or more accurately, sensuality. It's been said that men give tenderness in order to get sex, and women give sex in order to get tenderness. I have no idea whether that is true or not, but in healthy relationships we give tenderness in order to get tenderness.

74

What we need most

The life Bev and I have lived together has not been without its bumps and hollows, but here we are at our 50th anniversary and we are still in love. More importantly, we are still good friends. We enjoy being with each other. When we express our love to each other in the presence of our grandchildren, Bev and I are simply doing what comes naturally.

Zoë and Jake would know if we were play acting! We hope they will learn that it is possible for two people to love each other deeply and passionately, even when they are on the last lap of life's journey. We love the wrinkles in each other's faces, which are a testament to the Spirit's work in our lives.

As our grandchildren make us aware of how much we are filled and strengthened by their closeness, hugs, and intimacy, they can help us realize what it is we most fundamentally need from at least some of our adult relationships.

The expression of our love is as much a spiritual expression as any prayer or mantra or practice we may have at home or in our place of worship.

It's a kind of triangular relationship. Love God, love other people, love yourself.

Leave out one side of that triangle and life goes flat.

4

Laughing with Your Grandchildren

My grandmother had a delightful sense of humour.

As far as I know, she never told a joke nor got the point of one. My memory has her always in the midst of baking something. She would come and dust my nose with a bit of flour, then take me over to the mirror so we could laugh together.

I remember how surprised I was when she dusted my father's nose with flour. Dad had a pretty strong sense of personal dignity, and when Grandma did that I was hugely impressed.

Behind Grandma's house there was a small red barn that once held horses. She no longer kept horses, but the barn was full of interesting junk, including one of those large cardboard boxes in which bakeries used to ship bread to the stores.

Somehow Grandma, who was fairly round, got her backside into that box and couldn't get out. It struck her as funny and she started to laugh. The more she laughed, the deeper her bottom slid into the box. I don't remember how she got out, but of course she must have.

Grandma couldn't tell jokes, but she knew how to laugh at the scrapes and bumps of life.

If I would have known that grandchildren were going to be so much fun I would have had them first.

– VARIOUSLY ATTRIBUTED

Telling jokes

A sense of humour is a spiritual gift. And it has little to do with the ability to tell jokes. Joke telling is a theatrical skill and a fine one. But a sense of humour has more to do with an appreciation of the wonderful, holy, ludicrousness of life. "Humour," says author Conrad Hyers, "is not the opposite of seriousness. It is the opposite of despair."

The gift of humour is one of the most neglected. We don't think or talk about it much. We don't often wonder about our own sense of humour – what it means to us and how we use it – and so we're only dimly aware of its benefits and its dangers.

There's certainly tons of comedy around. Stand-up comics, sitcoms, political satirists, joke books. There's a whole TV channel showing wall-to-wall comedy.

But laughing at those is not the same as having a sense of humour. The comedy channel airs almost nothing but escapist humour. A vacation from reality. It's good and useful, unless it's a permanent escape. When the humour is violent and abusive – as it often is – then it is sick.

The gift of humour, like the gift of sex and like many of God's other greatest gifts, is often misused.

THE HUMOUR OF PARADISE

We can learn a lot from our grandchildren about the wonderful innocent humour small children are so good at. When I changed Zoë's diaper, I'd put my lips onto her tummy, blow, and make loud bubbly kinds of noises. Zoë would squeal with laughter.

One of my favourite humorous games is, "This little pig went to market…," which is done on the toes, complete with the wiggling of the smallest toe on, "wee, wee, wee, all the way home." You can do that over and over. You'll be worn out long before your grandchild. And of course there's the old standby, "Peek-a-boo!"

There are hundreds of wonderful little games and songs and poems like this. If your repertoire is a bit thin, talk to other grandparents. They will be delighted to tell you their favourites, along with their stories of how wonderful their grandchild is.

This primitive kind of humour is not clever. There is no real content to it. It requires no skill and no training. You don't have to be good at it. All it needs is one grandparent who loves one grandchild. If you just let your body and soul soak in the pure delight of it all, you may discover how deeply spiritual such play can be.

It's funny what happens when you become a grandparent. You start to act all goofy and do things you never thought you'd do. It's terrific.

~ Mike Krzyzewski

79

Conrad Hyers calls this kind of humour the humour of paradise. Totally innocent humour. It's the humour of infant Zoë living in the Garden of Eden, where she can squeal in delight when her grandpa makes funny faces and noises.

It's the humour of babies playing and babbling and simply enjoying life.

Jim Taylor was showing me pictures of his granddaughter, Katherine. The first pictures of her, taken in the orphanage in Ethiopia, showed a beautiful child, but her eyes were dull.

As we looked through the photos of Katherine taken subsequently, we could see the light growing in her eyes. The last photo showed Katherine, her head back, her eyes gleaming, in full laughter. Within the love of her new family, Katherine had discovered the humour of paradise.

Baby Katherine when we first met her at the orphanage in Ethiopia.

Now look at her!

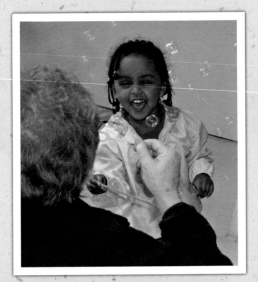

Paradise Lost

Katherine must leave the garden, of course. We all must leave. It is part of growing. In the old legend in the Bible, Eve and Adam eat the fruit that gives them the "knowledge of good and evil." We absolutely need, and we must cultivate, that knowledge of good and evil to live in human society. Animals don't need it. Humans do.

As babies grow, they discover that the world doesn't just exist to satisfy their needs for food and warmth and love. There are *other* people who have needs as well. Katherine will find that sometimes her needs and wants will conflict with the needs and wants of others. She will find that the world is a big, strange, often frightening place.

As Katherine leaves the garden of innocence, she will learn the humour of paradise lost. This is humour in the context of pain, confusion, anger, disappointment.

Hyers calls it "humour in the context of sin."

We joke about the parts of life that give us the most trouble — bodily wastes, sex, religion, power, family, aging, and health.

Anxiety about those areas stays with many people, especially men, well into adulthood, and sometimes throughout life. Our unresolved sexual issues give rise to all kinds of sexual humour, some of it vicious and degrading.

Humour about the areas of our anxiety can be very healthy. A good, genuinely funny joke or incident can help diffuse pain and anxiety.

But there are dangers.

DIRTY JOKES

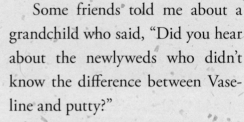

I have my own definition of a dirty joke. A joke is not dirty because it deals with sex. Sex is not dirty. It is one of God's great gifts and should be honoured. Treasured. It is sacramental. And it is good to laugh about it.

Some friends told me about a grandchild who said, "Did you hear about the newlyweds who didn't know the difference between Vaseline and putty?"

Granddad braced himself. "Ahhhh – no."

"Their windows fell out!" Which was screamingly funny to the child, who had no idea about the sexual aspect of the joke.

Then there was the grandmother who asked, "What did you talk about in school today?"

"Sex. But there's something I can't figure out."

"What is that?"

"Well, I know what they do. And how. But I can't figure out *why.*"

A dirty joke is one that has a victim. A good way to test whether a joke is dirty is to ask, "Who is not laughing?" It doesn't matter whether that person is present with you or not. Jokes that have victims reinforce our prejudice, our chauvinism, our anger. We especially should not tell victim jokes to our grandchildren, who will sense the negative value and may not know that it is wrong.

Another way of deciding whether a joke is dirty or not is to ask, "Are we laughing *at* someone, or *with* someone?"

There's a whole class of jokes that should be thrown in our cultural scrap heap. Polish jokes, Newfie jokes, dumb blond jokes, dumb men jokes – any joke that has a racial or gender or social victim. Some mother-in-law jokes can be particularly vicious.

Our task as grandparents is, first, to purge those jokes from our repertoire. Don't tell them anywhere to anyone. And let your friends know that those jokes are no longer acceptable.

The lone exception is when you tell jokes on yourself and those who are with you – when everybody present is the butt of the joke. I belong to a men's group where we often tell "dumb men" jokes on ourselves.

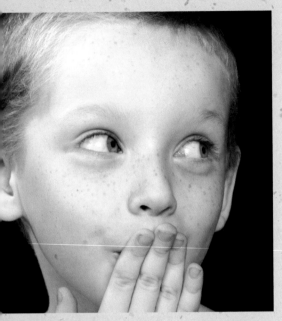

When a grandchild tells a joke with a victim, don't overreact. That might well have the effect of reinforcing the behaviour. But don't laugh either. The grandchild may give you some strange looks, but just quietly ask how the victim in the joke might have felt.

Don't overreact when you hear swearing, either. That usually makes the situation worse. But you *can* ask if the grandchild knows what the word means, and whether it's appropriate, or helps to make a point.

One grandma taught her grandson the word "scatological" and that it meant "stupid words about going to the bathroom." He was overheard saying to a small friend, "Don't talk scatological. My grandma doesn't like it."

Meg Hickling, author of *The New Speaking of Sex*, tells the story of a child who asked her the meaning of a certain word. Meg explained that it referred to sexual intercourse.

"That doesn't make sense," said the child. "When my mom slammed her finger in the car door, why would she say, 'Oh sexual intercourse'?"

Exactly. There are occasions and situations where a bit of mild profanity is useful and expressive. But most profanity is simply boring and shows that the user doesn't have much command of the language.

Which is a good thing to tell your grandchild. Swearing isn't so much bad as it is boring! There are lots of lively, expressive words in our language, words that communicate far more effectively than a small collection of four-letter profanities.

THE BENEFITS OF LAUGHTER

Laughter has important benefits for grandchildren and for grandparents alike. Laughing together creates special bonds and strengthens relationships. When we laugh together, we share something special with each other. We're both reacting to the same thing in the same way at the same time. At that moment, we're more alike than different. There is no generation gap. No one is "in charge." We're both on equal footing, laughing our heads off.

On top of that, laughter can improve learning, alleviate pain, speed recovery, and generally make us healthier physically and mentally. It's a no-cost little miracle. We often don't realize how important laughter is, and we don't do much to encourage it. But its presence or absence makes a big difference in the quality of our lives.

Please remember, though, that a sense of humour doesn't have much to do with the ability to tell jokes. A sense of humour has to do with seeing the bright nuggets of fun in life.

And it's great for relieving tension. Jim Taylor told me about his granddaughter, Katherine, who was being a little difficult about eating her dinner. In an angry reaction, Katherine managed to flip her bowl of food up in the air. It came back down on her head and all over the floor. Jim, Joan, and Sharon all broke into howls of laughter. Cleaning up Katherine and the floor was a whole lot easier than if they'd all been angry. And the child learned a valuable lesson about what is important and what isn't.

Children enjoy the fun of doing something ridiculous, or even slightly bad.

Never have I enjoyed youth so thoroughly as I have in my old age.

~ GEORGE SANTAYANA, *POET AND CRITIC*

Donna Scorer tells of being with her two grandchildren in their house one day when the parents were away. "Where would you like to eat dinner?" she asked them. "It can be anywhere in the house."

"On Mom and Dad's bed," came the immediate answer. So that's what they did. The children could hardly wait for the parents to get home so they could tell them.

And Tiffany, their mom, did exactly the right thing. "You did what?!" Later she said to Donna, "Why am I not surprised?"

Life is a laughing matter

Researchers have found that most adults laugh about 15 or 16 times a day. Toddlers laugh about 400 times a day. What happens as we grow older that we laugh so much less? And what can we do to help our grandchildren hang on to the joy and laughter that is so much a part of their early years?

It's really pretty easy. There are hundreds of ways to make grandchildren laugh. We only have to use some of them to make a difference in our grandchildren's lives and, coincidentally, in our own.

Start with your community library. There are lots of good humour books for every age. Video stores have movies with good fun in them. Most of all, talk to other grandparents to see what they've done.

This is not a new idea. The book of Proverbs, which comes to us from thousands of years ago, says, "A merry heart does good, like a medicine, but a broken spirit dries the bones."

Laughter is infectious. When you bring laughter into your grandchild's life, you bring it into your own.

Nobody can do for little children what grandparents do. Grandparents sort of sprinkle stardust over the lives of little children.

~ Alex Haley, *author*

LAUGH EARLY AND OFTEN

Grandchildren don't stay young forever, which is good because granddaddies have only so many horsy rides in them.

- GENE PERRET, *HUMOURIST*

Not surprisingly, your grandchild's sense of humour will change as he or she grows. Very young children, who still live at least partly in the garden of innocence, don't respond to clever humour. They respond best to physical comedy – to gestures, facial expressions, silly sounds, bouncing on Grandma's knee, flying in Grandpa's arms. Later, they're ready for simple funny games, like peek-a-boo and patty-cake. As grandparents, we seem to know instinctively what to do to make very young children laugh. Grandmas are usually better at this than we grandpas, but they can teach us old dogs some new tricks.

Toddlers and preschoolers have a sense of humour that is hard for most adults to understand. They think a duck in a cup or a cat in a tutu is hilarious. As they develop language skills, they play with words in ways that lead to peals of laughter.

Take, for instance, Jake's request for a glass of dinosaur juice. He thought he'd just asked for the funniest thing in the world, and so did I!

"Great idea! I think I'll have one too. I love dinosaur juice, almost as much as monkey milk."

Clever? No. Silly? Of course.

But it's important that grandparents laugh at their grandchildren's humour. Even when it doesn't strike you as all that funny. Your grandchildren need you to validate their humour. They also need to know that *you* have a sense of humour.

Until they are into the first year or two of school, grandchildren really don't understand jokes and riddles, but that doesn't keep them from trying their hand at them. Their attempts often don't make sense at all.

"Why did the chicken cross the street?" your granddaughter asks. Then she immediately answers her own question, "To get away from the dog," and dissolves in laughter. It's hard to join in with a belly laugh on that one, but join in as best you can.

Smile and say, "That's a good one. You really fooled me." One of these days she'll tell a joke that you'll also find funny, all because you appreciated her earlier efforts.

As children get a little older, it may get harder to laugh with them as their sense of humour becomes more sophisticated. But it's still very possible to find ways we can laugh together if we do some creative digging. There's a theatrical company in our town that specializes in old musical comedies – *Okalahoma, South Pacific, Brigadoon*. We take Jake and Zoë and their parents to the Saturday matinees. Enjoying the comedy and the music is a good way to use laughter to build bridges of love.

Paradise regained

I tend to be absent-minded. The day I poured buttermilk in my tea, Zoë, Jake, and I had a wonderful giggle over the way the tea curdled.

Rehearse funny family stories from time to time. "Do you remember the time Grandma Bev put salt in the apple crisp instead of sugar?" (But only do that when Grandma is there and can laugh with you.)

Don't be afraid to make a silly face or wear a silly hat or sing a silly song. If your grandkids have a dress-up box – a collection of old clothes and things to play dress-up with – join in. The kids will love it.

If your children don't have a dress-up box, go to a thrift store and buy a bunch of second-hand hats and gowns. The more outrageous, the better. Dig among your older clothes. A dress-up box makes a wonderful gift your grandchild will enjoy for years. And you can keep adding to it. Go back to that thrift shop and buy the most ridiculous item you can find and add it to their collection. Especially hats. Wearing a funny hat is an easy way to get everyone laughing.

Laughter really is the best medicine, as the *Reader's Digest* says. My late friend, Bob Hatfield, a medical doctor, often prescribed laughter as a good exercise. And it's true. A good belly-laugh, he told me, is "internal jogging" and releases as many endorphins into the brain as a handful of aspirin. A good belly-laugh also does much the same sort of thing, physiologically, as an orgasm. Which is great news at my age, because you can do it with anyone, anytime. And you can manage it more than once a month.

Children's laughter begins with the simple humour of paradise. They must grow up and leave the garden, and so spend most of their lives outside of paradise, where pain and anger and dishonesty prevail. A well-developed sense of humour will be of great benefit to them as they try to navigate through the rocks and eddies of life.

If we are lucky, we too can return to that simple, childlike humour. We can regain a touch of that paradise when we are old.

The humour of paradise regained comes to us only when we have nothing left to lose, when we've stopped trying to impress people. It's then that we can move back into the garden of paradise.

Should grandparents spoil? Every kid needs a bit of that.
The Bible is crammed with accounts of how God spoils us, that is, gives us better than we deserve.
It's called grace.

— STEPHEN AND JANET BLY,
AUTHORS

I saw that in my own grandma who lay on her bed and said to me, "I'm just waiting for my Jesus. And I wish he'd get on with it." I smiled at the tone of her voice, because she sounded the way she did when she'd tried to get me moving on some chores she had assigned.

I saw it in my friend Dorothy Barker, who was discharged twice from a hospice. "I guess God is still trying to figure out what to do with me," she joked.

No belly laughs. The humour of paradise regained is quiet and tender and can bring a tear as easily as it can bring a smile.

Near the heart of God

Very young grandchildren and very old grandparents share a precious gift that all the rest of us don't understand well. We can't. We have all the stuff of life swirling around us.

The very young are not yet bruised by the big and sometimes cruel world. They are newly given from the heart of God and are warmly wrapped in the small world of self and family.

The very old have set aside all the "stuff" that goes with trying to live creative lives and are content to have only the smallest circle of loved ones present. They feel the warm and loving hands of God reaching out to welcome them back home.

5

Long-Distance Grandparenting

"My grandma lives at the airport," said the four-year-old.

"How do you know that?" a friend asked.

"Well, when we want Grandma to visit, we go to the airport and get her. When we're finished having her visit, we take her to the airport and leave her there."

Back in the "good old days," if there ever was such a time, grandparents and grandchildren often lived in the same town. Often in the same house.

It's easy to get a bit dewy-eyed about that era. Do you remember the TV program *The Waltons,* where John-Boy and his siblings and his parents and his grandparents all lived in the same house, and they all got along so wonderfully and lovingly, and all said goodnight to each other as the lights went out around the house? We loved that program because that is how a family is supposed to be, even though it hardly ever is.

Always there is that sense of belonging to the larger human community where, in spite of differences there are memories of earlier grandparents that resonate, because we, too, have our own memories of that stern or loving – or both – older man or woman who sat at the head of the Thanksgiving table, presided over a family gathering, or offered a consoling word during a childhood crisis.

– James Wall

By the time I came along, the youngest in the family, we had only one grandparent left – my grandmother on my mother's side of the family. I have wispy childhood memories of travelling to her house. She lived about ten miles away, a great distance in those days. Grandma always had peppermint candies in her pocket. They smelled a bit like mothballs.

But in her later years, she was moved every month or so from house to house among her children, and I know from what my mother told me that this was not an easy or happy solution for Grandma or for her children.

I remember her sitting on a chair under a tree in our backyard. She would sometimes pluck a leaf from a nearby bush and eat it. She'd shudder and grimace at the taste of it. If I was watching, she would recite a short German poem that said the worse something tastes the better it is for you. If she came upon a leaf that was so bitter she could hardly stand it, she would immediately pluck another leaf and eat it. I guess that's where I got my idea that medicine must never taste good.

Eventually, Grandma was placed in the "Old Folks Home," as they used to call it. I don't know if that was better or worse. I remember her lying on her bed with a large bottle of Wonder Oil at her bedside. It was just as well she couldn't read the English label. She would have been horrified if she'd known it was 25 percent alcohol. But it made her feel better, so my mother never told her what was in it.

Our children didn't really know their grandparents. When our son Mark was two and our daughter Kari was three months old, we moved to the Philippines. We were sent to help the churches of the Philippines use radio to do community development and education.

It was the only time I saw my father-in-law cry. I saw his face as we waved out the train window. I'm sure he thought we were taking his grandchildren to the end of the world, and that he'd never see them or us again.

Soon after we returned from the Philippines, we moved to Teaneck, New Jersey. Bev's parents lived way on the other side of the continent, in Victoria, British Columbia. Her mother died during that time. My mother lived in Winnipeg. If it had not been for "Auntie Frances," our four children would not have known what a real live grandparent was like.

Things got a bit better when we moved back to Canada, but the visits were still sporadic. My mother hated travelling by air and the bus wore her out. Travelling was also very expensive.

Bev and I are incredibly fortunate. Our grandchildren live close enough that we can get together often, but not so close that we're always on each other's laps.

The bad news and the good news

The bad news is that improvements in air transport and an increasingly international economy means the situation is getting worse. Friends here in western Canada have a grandchild in Germany. That's not unusual.

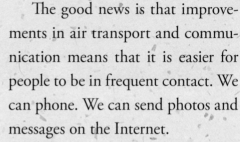

The good news is that improvements in air transport and communication means that it is easier for people to be in frequent contact. We can phone. We can send photos and messages on the Internet.

And we can travel far more easily and cheaply than previous generations. Yes, airfares have gone up, but in relation to our standard of living they have gone down. Most people are able to travel far more often than they ever thought possible. Our friend with the grandchildren in Germany flies over there at least every year or two.

Still, things are not likely to get better.

It doesn't help to sit around and wring your hands and feel sorry for yourself. And it usually doesn't help to move closer to where your kids are, because the average family moves once every five years. So they're fairly likely to move somewhere else after you get there.

Whenever we go to visit our grandkids, Bev and Kari haul out the date books and look weeks and months ahead to find times when we can fit into their busy lives. One of the benefits of living close is that we are able to go to many of the events in which the grandkids are involved – school concerts, church events, ballet recitals, and band concerts. But it takes planning.

There's also the danger of unrealistic expectations. Families, most of them with two parents working outside the home and children involved in all sorts of activities, often don't want Grandma and Grandpa underfoot all the time.

It hurts

In preparing for this book, I started an Internet online group to discuss grandparenting issues and to share ideas. They were a lively bunch from about five different countries.

Ruth Zenger, one of the members, wrote

Living across the country from my two oldest grandchildren has meant we have never been an important part of their lives.

This far-flung family has just lost their grandfather and will now never know him any better than through their past sporadic times together. I think the lack of contact is a greater loss for the grandchildren than for the grandparents. It is just that we know what we are missing and they do not – until too late.

In the same on-line discussion group, Jim Taylor wrote

I too would love to see our granddaughter more often. She lives an 11-hour drive away from us. I realize now – 30 years too late – how my parents might have felt.

They lived in Vancouver; we lived in Toronto, almost 5,000 kilometres away. Crossing the country was a major trip back then, by car or by plane. Joan's parents rarely travelled. They saw their grandchildren only when we came west on holidays.

And my own grandparents must have felt even more cut off. Because my parents were missionaries, my mother's parents only saw me every seventh year, when my parents came "home" on furlough. I can't help feeling a loss. For all grandparents and grandchildren kept apart by circumstances beyond their control.

Janet Koschzeck in Naramata, British Columbia, wrote

Quite recently I began to think of my own parents leaving their families behind in England when we emigrated in 1947. We never saw our grandparents again!

Then, because my husband was in the military for over 20 years, my parents didn't see our four children for three years. I can't remember hearing them ever complain. But I do complain, often, when we're unable to see our first and maybe only granddaughter in Victoria!

In the meantime, we exchange letters, artwork, photos, and phone calls, as well as scrapbooks.

There are ways of making long-distance connections that forge the vital links — so that grandparents and grandchildren are not strangers when they meet, but loving relations who have found ways to transcend the miles that keep them physically apart.

– Selma Wassermann, *The Long Distance Grandmother*

One of the gifts of age is that we have a long perspective. Most of us have dealt with many difficult situations in our lives, and we have survived.

I talked to many grandparents as I prepared this book, most of them long-distance grandparents. As I listened to the ways they adapted to their situation, I noticed that the essential ingredients in their relationship with their grandchildren are creativity, patience, and risk. These people think outside the box. They entertain wild and wonderful ideas about how they and their grandchildren can do more than tell each other what the weather is like where they live.

For instance, a grandparent I met at an Elderhostel program told me he e-mailed his grandkids telling them he would phone on a certain evening, and that he would ask them questions about what happened in school, and is the cold they had last week getting better, and did they get invited to their friend's birthday party? And he asked them to send him e-mails with questions so that he could be ready.

"That means I have to do a bit of work to keep track of what's going on in their lives," he grinned.

If your memory is as leaky as mine, you'll need to take lots of notes. I rely on Bev far too much to keep track of such things for me.

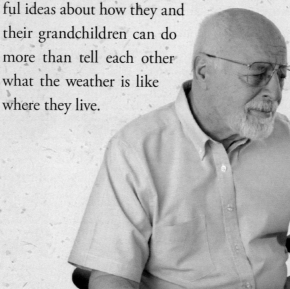

Many grandparents – maybe most of them – have learned to use the media. They have a fine time sending messages and photographs to their grandkids. Some of them have a little video camera on top of their computer, so they can see each other while they talk.

Most communities offer a variety of computer courses too. Our community college has held special sessions for seniors. Grandkids these days have known about computers and cell phones and all the electronic doodads all their lives and they can help us cope with these newfangled gizmos, if we ask them. Believe it or not, many of these electronic contraptions are actually becoming easier to operate.

And don't ever let anyone tell you that you can't teach an old dog new tricks. Recent research has shown that our brains retain much of their ability to learn as we get older. A cover story in *Maclean's* magazine titled "The Secret to Not Losing Your Marbles" quotes Dr. Michael Merzenich of Yale University. "You *can* learn to play the piano if you are 70. The brain is plastic through a lifetime." Our brains need exercise, just like any other part of our body.

PATIENCE

Don't give up easily. Especially on yourself and on new communication devices. It's easy to feel intimidated by them. Except for the telephone, most of the electronic media we now take for granted hadn't even been dreamt of when we were kids.

So it's easy to sit around feeling stupid. But try not to. Be gentle with yourself. If the geekish teenager trying to teach you how to use a computer has a long-suffering, exasperated look on his face, find someone else. You may not understand computers, but you know other stuff it will take him a lifetime to learn.

If your grandkids don't respond to your e-mail, do something really innovative. Send an old-fashioned snail-mail letter. The last I heard, the post office still handled those. Just because something doesn't work the first time doesn't mean you give up. Do a bit of tweaking and then try again.

GIFT GIVING

It's important to be creative around gift giving. It's useful to think a little about what you really want from your grandchildren and what they really need from you.

Our son Mark asked Jake and Zoë for a "work of art I can hang on my wall." He made it clear he didn't want refrigerator art. He wanted them to sit down and do the very best picture they could manage, and he wanted it framed. The picture was a gift from them to him; the request was a gift from him to them.

Their Aunt Elo once gave the gift of a "special day." She spent a day with Zoë and Jake and their cousins individually. "Anywhere you want to go and anything you want to do. Within reason, of course." In the process, they enjoyed some quality time together.

Grandma Bev and Zoë

Bev and Zoë have dolls who are friends. Zoë's doll Katie and Bev's doll Joanne go to visit each other. Joanne once stayed with Katie when we went on a trip. One Christmas there were gifts from one doll to the other.

Bev's doll is named Joanne, because that is her second given name. "She represents the child in me," says Bev. Zoë is rapidly growing out of the age when children play a lot with dolls, but I have a feeling – or at least I hope – that through the years she will allow her inner child, Katie, to play with her grandmother's inner child, Joanne.

And when Bev passes on, Joanne will go to be with Katie. Throughout her life, Zoë will remember Grandma Bev through those dolls.

The best gifts are always those that involve giving of the self. It's so easy picking up another "thing" at the nearest toy superstore, which meets the obligation to send something for the birthday or other occasion. But an important aspect of spiritual grandparenting is the sharing of ourselves – a sharing that is best when it happens in two directions. It takes more work and imagination, but these kinds of investments pay off in the long run.

RISK

Reaching out to your grandchildren is risky. It could backfire. Then the only thing to do is to ask for a direct and clear response about what was not appreciated, and hope that you get an honest answer. Ask their parents for suggestions.

Your grandkids and their parents need to know, however, that you're not going to stomp off in a huff. When one thing doesn't work, go on to something else.

Get help. Organize a grandparents group. You could do that through your church, or through your community organizations or senior citizens' group. Stand up on your hind legs and say it loudly and clearly. "I need help! I need help staying in touch with my grandchildren. I want to meet with a group of other long-distance grandparents so we can swap ideas and give each other suggestions."

This could develop into a group of friends with whom you could have a bang-up Grandparents' Day celebration (see Chapter 7).

We can go into a quiet retirement, which is the traditional stereotype of a 65-year-old, or we can take a risk and put ourselves out where the action is.

~ Satenig St. Marie

Hanna Tennenhaus couldn't understand what the fuss was all about. The 83-year-old grandmother found herself famous in the computer world, even though she doesn't own a computer.

Her grandson, Shmuel, videotaped Hanna's New Year's greetings. Hanna thought they were just for her four children, 16 grandchildren, and 32 great-grandchildren.

But Shmuel sent the video to *YouTube* (I had to ask my grandkids what that was) and they featured it on their home page. Within a few days, her greeting had been seen more than 210,000 times. And that generated dozens of phone calls.

When Hanna finally got to see the video herself, she was astounded. "That's it? That's it? And that goes around the world? They're crazy!"

Surrogate grandparenting

I mentioned the blessing that "Auntie Frances" was to our children when we lived in New Jersey, so far away from their grandparents. Among the most useful things some grandparents have done is to encourage just this kind of surrogate grandparenting.

"It was a little hard to do," I was told by a grandmother who didn't want her name used.

I felt a little jealous sometimes. But my grandchildren needed someone who was right there, so I suggested to my kids that they try to find such a surrogate grandparent. Well, it turns out their church had a "secret pen-pal" program where they connected seniors and children. And that's how they found a granddad for my grandchildren.

The neatest thing is that he's kind of acting as my spy. He phones me and tells me what's happening with my grandchildren and often suggests things I can do with them.

So I asked this grandmother, "Are you going to find some surrogate grandchildren of your own? It seems to me you have lots of grandmother love to spare?"

She thought for a moment. "I just might do that. And if I can find a child or two that are the same age as my grandchildren, I'll know better what's going on with kids that age."

A child needs a grandparent, anybody's grandparent, to grow a little more securely into an unfamiliar world.

~ Charles and Ann Morse, *AUTHORS*

In her book *Wells of Wisdom*, Maren Tirabassi, who pastors a congregation in New Hampshire, describes herself as a "grandparent-in-waiting." But one night she had a dream.

When I woke up in the morning, I realized that I am called to be a grandparent *now*. My role as grandparent is tied not to the biology of my children but to my commitment to nurture the "two down" generation. It is a "call." All of us codgers and crones are called not to wait or be selective but to give to the children around us in that rich way that really cannot be imitated by anyone in the responsible generation – the job-tending, bill-paying, car-driving, video-renting, earache-waking, report-card-locating responsible generation.

What grandparents can give is unique, and in a social milieu where distance and divorce and even the stretching out of generations may interfere with, postpone, or alter biologically oriented grandparent-grandchild relationship, there is no lack of children that need that love.

Long-distance grandparenting is hardest when grandchildren are very young. They often don't remember us from one visit to the next. We want and expect to be welcomed with open arms, but the grandchild cries and hides behind a parent. It's painful to realize that we're a stranger to our grandchild, whom we love so much.

That's when we simply have to swallow hard, breathe deeply, and be patient. Give the child lots of time to study you from a safe distance, and after a while you'll have that child in your arms again.

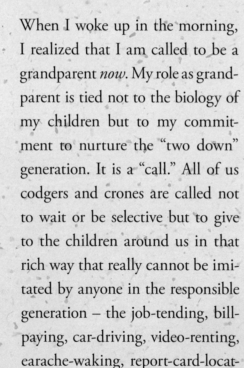

Overcompensating

A big mistake many grandparents make is to be a bit too demonstrative with their affection. To have someone shower you with kisses and hugs may be terrifying for a young child, especially if the youngster doesn't normally get that sort of treatment from their parents or other adults.

The other tendency we have is to overcompensate when it comes to giving gifts. We naturally feel a bit guilty about having spent the winter down in Arizona or Florida, so we load up the kids with mounds of toys and cute clothes. We may do the same thing at Christmas and for birthdays.

This causes two problems. First, excessive gifts do not make your grandchildren love you more. In fact, they may come to think of you primarily as a walking toy store. Gifts are never a substitute for anything, especially not for time spent with your grandchild. The old adage is really true: "You can't buy love."

Second, it's not good for children to have too many toys. Aside from making their bedrooms look like a junky used-toy store, they become jaded. Nothing excites them anymore. They don't know what it is to yearn for something. To want something badly. To earn something.

The simplest toy, one which even the youngest child can operate, is called a grandparent.

~ Sam Levenson,
HUMOURIST AND JOURNALIST

LONG-DISTANCE STORY TIME

I heard recently of a creative grandmother who read to her grandchild every night on the phone. She worked hard to find the right kinds of books: books that were well-written and yet entertaining, books that had something worthwhile to say. She always consulted with the parents on this.

If there are pictures in the book, I buy two copies and send one to my grandson. My daughter has arranged for a speaker phone beside his bed so that he can manage the pages. It turns out the speaker phone was as much for her as for her child. She wanted to listen too. And there's usually a conversation after the story reading.

As for the long-distance phone charges – well a bit of research revealed a number of ways to reduce that cost. Anyway, who can put a price on it?

Tasting the tradition

Food can be an important part of long-distance grandparenting.

When I was a young bachelor living far from home, my mother would send me a "care package" every year before Christmas, and it always contained oatmeal-date cookies. My favourite. They not only tasted wonderful, they reminded me of my family and home, and would often prompt a letter. Phone calls were reserved for emergencies in those days.

Taste and smell are the most primitive of our senses, and have deep emotional connections, so it's good to be as traditional as possible. But it's also good to check once in a while to make sure that what you're sending is actually appreciated.

One grandmother wrote about how devastated she was. She had been sending her grand-children packages of her Ukrainian perogies every year, only to discover later, when they were adults, that they all *hated* perogies. It's wise to check our assumptions.

Many religious traditions involve food. This is particularly rich in Jewish culture, where the family gathered around the table for the Sabbath meal is central to the practice of that faith.

Boiled eggs, as a symbol of new life, are an important part of many Easter celebrations. Somehow, chocolate eggs in foil wrap just don't carry the message.

I could make my grandmother go into raptures of joy, just by being hungry.

– Jean-Paul Sartre, PHILOSOPHER

Elizabeth Wong writes:

I'm Chinese. I married a Norwegian. Our son's wife is a Filipina. All of us grew up on this continent, so we've already lost most of our distinct cultures. Children of mixed races tend to be beautiful and our granddaughter is gorgeous. But culturally, she's a kind of bland North American. Her cultural food would be a hamburger.

It's a two-hour plane flight from our house to theirs, but once a year we get together for a week, and during that week we celebrate five special days.

We have Christmas – with all the gifts happening then, not on December 25 – complete with turkey and all the trimmings. We celebrate Easter, too, with ham and boiled eggs and an Easter egg hunt.

And then we have our three major ethnic festivals. We do Norwegian *Tyvendedagen*, for which my husband gets some *lutefisk*. My granddaughter hates it, but she eats a bit for Grandpa's sake. We have Chinese New Year, and I break out the dried oysters, garlic, ginger – the works. And we have Philippine Independence Day, for which we do *lechon*. Well, not the whole roast pig, but a nice pork roast.

And often we talk about the spiritual heritage we grew up with – what we want to hang on to and what we want to leave behind.

So we have a whole year of festivals in one week and it is a riot. Otherwise, we would celebrate those feast days alone, which is no fun at all.

It helps our granddaughter sense a bit of her rich heritage.

Keeping up

Time seems to speed up as we get older. We don't see our grandchildren for a while, and when we see them next they seem to have grown a foot.

Keeping up with clothing sizes is hard enough, but keeping up with their growing minds is even harder. Like physical growth, emotional and intellectual growth comes in spurts. If you've not seen your grandchild for a while, even if you've been in contact on the phone, it's good to ask one of the parents for a briefing. The flat-chested granddaughter who was playing with Barbie dolls the last time you visited may be wearing a brassiere and noticing boys.

The last time Bev and I came back from a month in the Arizona sun I heard a distinct huskiness in Jake's voice. He says he had a cold, but I'm not convinced. One of these days our boy soprano may be a basso-profundo.

It is at times like this that a grandparent may be able to initiate unique celebrations to mark the passages of life. Traditional cultures almost always had a ceremony to mark the beginning of adulthood. In Jewish custom, it is the *bar mitzvah* when the boy is 13, and now more and more the *bat mitzvah* for girls when they are 12.

Celebrations of the change from child to adult can also follow the more natural rhythms of the body – the first menstruation for girls, or the change of voice for boys. But always, always consult with the parents before you initiate anything.

CUTTING THE CORD

The physical umbilical cord is cut at birth, but cutting the spiritual/psychological umbilical cord takes much longer and is more painful. Even now, more than half a century since my father died, I find myself wondering what he might think of me and of what I am doing.

As children become teenagers and then young adults, they need to move away from their parents and their grandparents. Most of us have experienced some of that as parents – knowing our children must leave, wanting them to leave, pushing them out the door – yet wanting desperately to hold them back, because we know they are not ready. And we are not ready either. Perhaps we never will be.

At the very least, as grandparents we need to do whatever we can to support the parents through this sometimes difficult transition.

Roots and wings

That's the hardest thing. Letting go. Grandchildren may not want to visit Grandma and Grandpa for a while. That's really hard on us, but we simply have to face up to it.

Bev has memories of living with her grandmother while going to university. It was necessary to save money. But it wasn't a completely happy arrangement. Among other things, she was expected to visit her other grandmother every Saturday, which certainly cut down on her social life. I don't think Bev really regrets it now, but at the time she was unhappy about it.

I'm not sure which would be tougher – living close to our grandchildren all their growing-up years and then seeing them go off to work or school, and becoming long-distance grandparents. Or having lived some distance away from them knowing that they are leaving their nest and that we'll have even less contact with them in the years ahead.

It's been said that parents must give their children two gifts. Roots and wings. Deep roots in family love and spirituality. Strong wings to fly away, to discover their Creator's dream for them, and then fly back home when they are ready. A part of those gifts come from spiritual grandparents.

There may come a time when we must say to our grandchild, "You may not want to come around and see me for a while. That's okay. I didn't want to visit my grandparents either when I was your age. Just remember that wherever your life takes you, I will still love you. And when you feel you'd like to come and visit me, I'll be waiting with open arms."

Although [grandparents] may have looked like parents at first, they lived in a third universe where there was less chance of error, where this ground had been covered long before and the wisdom of age brought freedom for adult and child.

– Muriel Duncan,
JOURNALIST

A grandmother in Montreal sent this note:

I have two candles I light on our dinner table. I light them each evening. I light the green one to remember Joel, because green was always his favourite color. And I light the purple one to remember Andrea. Purple was her favourite.

I say a prayer for them as I light the candles, asking God to be with them in whatever they are doing, and to give them strength to make wise choices. I send them pictures of the candles every Christmas, along with my Christmas letter.

Joel phones me every once in a while, but I haven't heard from Andrea for two years and that worries and pains me. But I will keep lighting the candles and praying.

THE LONG-DISTANCE NORM

I have no surveys that I can quote, but I am quite sure that most grandparents relate to their grandchildren over a distance. The old poem, "Over the river and through the woods, to Grandmother's house we go," describes a time gone by. Grandma doesn't live there anymore. She's practising law in Regina.

Maybe such a time never existed. Sixty years ago when I was cutting that umbilical cord, my parents and others worried about all the things that were threatening family life.

We're still saying much the same things. Is family life disappearing? Are grandparents a kind of cultural holdover from a bygone era? Are we social dinosaurs?

I don't think so. Long-distance grandparenting is difficult, often frustrating, and expensive. But if we approach it joyfully and creatively – if we keep good communication going with our children and their partners – it can continue to nourish the spirits of both grandchildren and grandparents.

The love – the spiritual link we have with our grandchildren – can overcome any distance.

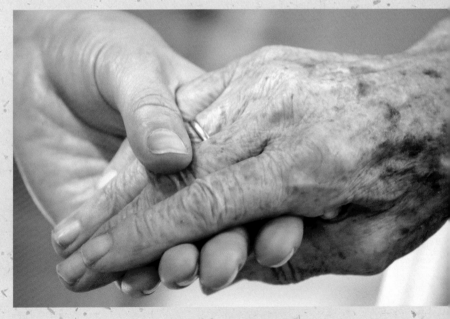

6

Leaving a Legacy

I don't know how it began. But I'll not soon forget a conversation with my granddaughter Zoë, now a ten-year-old almost woman. It was long and leisurely – about everything and nothing.

Zoë talked about what she wanted to do with her life – be an author, write children's stories. "Stories that help explain things for kids, and maybe funny stories too."

Zoë was all smiles when I told her the best training to be an author is to read, which she just loves. We talked about my childhood, my journey. About family who lived and people who died. And why people have to die.

No, I didn't preach her any little sermons. This was a dialogue, a person-to-person conversation – adult-to-adult actually.

Zoë may not remember the moment, but I will. Because that evening I lay in bed and I knew the miracle of seeing deeply into the life of a person I love most dearly – of seeing in this child the fine, made-in-the-image-of-God woman she is becoming.

And I prayed that she would have the courage, the strength, to wrestle the dark angels that wait along her pathway. And perhaps, just perhaps, at the end of the first decade of her life, she saw into the heart of a made-

I am your heritage and you are my legacy. We are part of a chain. Come to me for the wisdom of my experience and for my love that knows no bounds. Let me come to you for the newness of your experience and for your love that knows no bounds.

– Arthur Kornhaber,
author

in-the-image-of-God grandpa, who is quite possibly in the last decade of his life.

Perhaps she will pray that I have the courage, the strength, to wrestle the dark angels that wait along my pathway.

And maybe. Just maybe, Zoë and I will have such conversations again.

More than money

I'd like to leave a legacy for Zoë and Jake. I'm not talking about money. If there's any left when I die, it will soon be spent and forgotten.

Every once in a while, when Jake or Zoë has done or said something delightful, son-in-law Don will smile and say, "Just like Grandma Bev," or "Sure takes after you, Grandpa." He intends it as a compliment, and it's music to our ears.

We all would like to believe that there is something good in us that we have passed on to the next generation. It's a kind of immortality, I expect. Or at least I hope. I'd really like to see my grandchildren become adults and move out into the world. It's not likely I'll be around much longer than that. But I like to think that part of me is in their bodies, their minds, their souls, that they in turn will leave as a legacy to their children and their grandchildren. It's nothing specific or tangible that I can put my finger on. But it's there, nonetheless.

Is it nature or nurture? In other words, that part of ourselves that we want to pass on to our grandchildren – is it in the genes or is it something they absorb from the family and culture in which children grow?

WHO ARE WE?

Have you seen the musical *Fiddler on the Roof*? In the opening scene, Tevye talks about his Jewish traditions. "We have traditions for the way we sleep, the way we do our work, the clothes we wear and the food we eat. Because of our traditions, we know who we are and what God expects us to do."

Perhaps the greatest Jewish tradition is the Sabbath. The way the Sabbath is observed varies with different groups within the Jewish community, but all of them treat it as a special day, different from all the other days of the week. I've heard it said that the Jews did not preserve the Sabbath. The Sabbath preserved the Jews.

When we lived in New Jersey, we had Jewish friends with whom we shared many of our religious festivals. Naomi and Isaac Goldstein were committed and observant Jews, but they were also eager to share the richness of our traditions. And so they invited us to share the Passover Seder with them, and we invited them to our house to share Christmas with us.

"I want the Christmas story straight up," said Naomi, who described herself as a *Yiddishe mama*. "None of your be-nice-to-the-Jews stuff."

So our Christmas with the Goldsteins was more religious than when we celebrated on our own. And the Jewish festivals we shared with them had none of the be-nice-to-the-Christians stuff in them either.

Isaac sold high-tech medical equipment around the world. I asked him once, "How do you manage to observe the Sabbath when you are in a hotel in Tokyo, for instance."

"It's very hard," he said. "It sure would be more convenient to just forget about the whole thing. And I often argue with myself. So, would it be such a terrible thing if you ate a ham sandwich or went to a meeting instead of doing your pitiful Sabbath thing all alone in your hotel room? There are times I've done that. I've said to heck with it. But whenever I do, I feel less of a person. I feel like my heart has gone dead in me."

Isaac was talking about his spiritual centre. He knew how inconvenient and unpopular it often was to protect and nourish his spiritual centre, which was grounded in his Jewish faith and expressed through that tradition. "But my kids know who they are," he said with evident pride. "They know they are different and sometimes they kvetch about it. But sometimes they also know how valuable it is."

Building a tradition

When Jake and Zoë came along, I built them an Advent house. It's a house front with many doors. Each year, four weeks before Christmas, Bev and I deliver the Advent house. Every morning during the four weeks leading up to Christmas, the children open one of the doors and discover something their Grandma Bev has put there. It may be a saying or a riddle or an activity or a symbol. And on Christmas morning, the first thing they do is open the main door, the Christmas door of the Advent house.

On Christmas Eve day, Bev and I arrive at their home. We share the gifts we have for each other. Last year we took an hour to look at a series of slides about our family. We may make that an annual event.

Then we have Christmas dinner together. But not your standard Christmas dinner. Jake and Zoë get to choose the menu, and for the last several years it's been Kraft Dinner.

Then we go to the Christmas Eve service at their church. I like it best when they offer the age-old and familiar Bethlehem story. The year Zoë was born in mid-December, Kari and Don played the part of Mary and Joseph, and Zoë was the baby Jesus.

The Advent House

I wanted to be sure to get pictures of this great event, so I walked down the centre aisle looking for a seat. Four teenage girls were sitting near the end of a pew. "Could you move over just a bit?" I asked them. "I want to take pictures. I'm Jesus' grandfather." The girls gave me an odd look and moved as far over as they could.

Zoë as the baby Jesus with her mom and dad

Kari and Don have worked hard to establish and build rich family traditions. Not only around the religious holidays like Christmas and Easter, but in everyday things. For example, they say grace before their meals, but when we come to visit, they sing, "For the beauty of the earth, for the glory of the skies…" Nothing quiet or meditative about this. The guys – Don, Jake and I – sing out with great gusto. In the last two lines of the verse, Grandpa breaks into harmony and Zoë cringes at the sound of it all. The singing, the harmony and the cringe are all part of the family tradition.

Singing grace

Choosing traditions

If the old will remember, the very young will listen.

– Chief Dan George

Some of us, like the Goldsteins, have a rich ethnic and religious heritage to observe and to celebrate. But I'm not suggesting that we observe everything in our heritage. We need to discard those traditions that are hurtful and cruel. Or that are no longer meaningful. And then we need to work hard to celebrate the traditions we have chosen, because they can quite easily be buried – overwhelmed by the consumer culture that rolls over us every time we turn on the TV or go to the mall.

It's harder to have traditions when people from different cultures marry each other. Bev's family was English and Alsatian. Mine was Russian Mennonite. Don's family roots are Scottish. So what kind of a tradition do my grandchildren have?

As grandparents, we can encourage and help our children choose and develop the traditions that will feed and nourish our grandchildren. There are traditional foods we can make for special occasions, or we can pass along the recipe. There are songs we can teach, and stories we can tell – particularly stories of how we remember things from our childhood days.

Parents, aunts, uncles, cousins – all can describe traditions from their culture. Are there some traditions you can bring up from the past to enrich your present?

In the first chapter I told the story of Rabbi Wosk and the glass of water. He spoke of his traditions as the container, the vessel, in which he held his religious convictions.

The traditions we bring from the past to enrich our present are not just fun things to do. They should be pleasurable, yes, but they also provide a way we can celebrate and affirm, in the words of Tevye, "who we are and what God expects us to do."

Our traditions – the ones we bring from the past and the ones we invent – are the vessels of our spirituality.

The power of grandparent stories to transmit values, traditions, wisdom and love are felt throughout a child's life.

– S. KANDEL, *AUTHOR*

It is particularly in the Negro spirituals that my parents and grandparents gave me "food" for my journey.

– GILBERT H. CALDWELL, *PASTOR*

In many traditions, especially among First Nations people, the grandparents are the storytellers. It is their responsibility to bring the wisdom of the past into the present for the benefit of the grandchildren.

Flora Wilson Bridges, speaking at a conference in Victoria, British Columbia, noted the key role grandparents play in the African-American community. Grandparents, she said, are the ones given the most authority – even more than the parents – because they have survived against all challenges. It's the grandparent's role, Flora emphasized, to nurture a sense of group identity, and to pass on the wisdom necessary for survival.

There are many things we can do in our role as the "keeper of the flame." But we need to learn how to do this without being a bore – without turning off our grandkids and their parents. If we don't do it carefully and thoughtfully, those traditions will go to the grave with us.

Every situation is different. So here are a number of things others have done. Maybe just reading these ideas will inspire you to something original, tailor-made just for your grandchildren. If so, be sure to share it with other grandparents.

These are all little things. If we do these kinds of things often, our grandkids will absorb a surprising amount of our family legacy.

❧ When we are cooking or cleaning out the garage, we can sing the songs we remember from our childhood, even if they are in a language our grandchildren don't understand. You'd be surprised how much children pick up when we think they're not listening. Eventually, perhaps after hearing them many times, they may ask us what the songs are about.

❧ When a grandchild celebrates a birthday, we can send an old picture of ourselves or of someone in our extended family when they were the same age. On the phone or in a note, we can tell them a bit of the story of that person and of how she or he is connected to our grandchild.

❧ We can look for moments when a certain behaviour or characteristic or habit in our children or our grandchildren reminds us of someone in our family history. "The way you laugh reminds me so much of your father!" Or, "My grandma made me a dress like that once!"

❧ It's good to drive past the old family home or other landmarks whenever there's an opportunity. Or send a picture. "See that tree? I planted that. It was just a tiny sapling this high. Now look at it!"

❧ I like to tell stories, especially funny stories, about myself and my family. The hardest part for me is to include only the details that are necessary to understand the story. On more than one occasion, I've seen eyes glaze over around the dinner table, and I know old "motormouth" grandpa is being a bore.

❧ Let's not wait until we die to pass on family heirlooms. When a grandson's voice begins to change or a granddaughter has her first menstruation (check with the parents about this first!), we can celebrate their movement into adulthood with a gift from our past. A grandchild's going off to college might be a good time to pass along an old slide rule. "This was the computer, the calculator we used. I know your granddad would want you to have it." When I got married, I received my dad's wedding ring.

✽ Thank goodness Bev does this, because I'd never get around to it. She keeps those photo albums in order. And she labels the pictures. Our grandchildren don't give them a second look right now, but when they are 55 with grandchildren of their own…

✽ Recipes. Just family favourites, including traditional dishes. We need to put them into a form so that when our grandchildren start cooking, those recipes will be there for them.

✽ Share photos from time to time. But just one or two every now and then. I bought a digital camera that lets me take a batch of photos and there's no extra cost. That's good news and bad news. I try hard to only save the really good photos. But I already have over a thousand on my computer and that's way too many.

If God had intended us to follow recipes, [God] wouldn't have given us grandmothers.

– Linda Henley, *HUMOURIST*

There's a story about a grandmother who told her granddaughter what her childhood was like. "We used to skate outside on a pond," she said. "I had a swing made from a tire that hung from a tree in our front yard. We rode our pony. We picked tiny, sweet wild strawberries in the woods."

The granddaughter was wide-eyed. "Gee, Grandma," she said. "I sure wish I'd gotten to know you sooner!"

Among the writing courses I've taught was one on how and why you might write your autobiography.

But I always begin with some reasons why you should *not* write your autobiography. If you are expecting to have it published or that it will bring you fame and fortune, you will probably be disappointed. An autobiography usually brings fame and fortune only to those who already have fame and fortune.

There are two reasons why you *should* write your life story.

First, retirement is the Sabbath of life. It is the time to reflect on who you are, on who you have been, and on the meaning of your life. Writing your life story will help you do that.

Second, it is a way of leaving your legacy to those who come after you. "My grandchildren aren't interested in my life story," people sometimes say to me. "Probably not now," I say. "Especially not if they are teenagers. But when they get older, they'll be interested. They'll want a sense of where they came from so they can understand who they are. You simply have to trust the future."

WORTH REMEMBERING

A few years ago I saw a delightful letter from a man who rented a community hall for a long weekend. He invited his children, his grandchildren, and assorted aunts and uncles and cousins, and asked them to bring all their memorabilia with them, including boxes of old photos. He describes what happened next.

I got this big roll of newsprint from the local newspaper office and I put it up, right around all four walls of the community hall. Then I marked years on it – starting from a hundred years ago and working up to the present.

I put up tables all over the place, with typewriters and rolls of masking tape. When the whole gang arrived, we had a marvellous chaos of putting names to old photos, arguing about what happened when, and sitting down at a typewriter and writing a story we suddenly remembered. We pasted the photos and stories at the appropriate spot on the newsprint. Even the youngest grandchildren got into it.

Now I've got this huge roll of newsprint beside me. It smells of take-out Chinese food and pizza, and it's my job to put this into some kind of a book. But I want you to know it was one of the best weekends of my life.

The four symbolic functions of a grandparent: Being There, Family National Guard, Family Arbitrator, Autobiographer.

– V. L. BENGSTON, *AUTHOR*

If the idea of writing your autobiography doesn't excite you, there are alternatives.

Garth Fletcher, a friend in Pittsburgh, didn't want to do his own writing. So he went to a local university and talked to one of the instructors who taught a writing class. Through that instructor, Garth was able to contact a student who spent many hours with him, interviewing him about his life's story. Then the student wrote it into a book, which Garth corrected and fixed as necessary. When they were done, they had a few copies made for relatives and friends. Garth, of course, paid the student. "It was worth it!" he said. "I never could have done that myself."

Scrapbooks are a good idea. You can include all sorts of pictures and newspaper clippings, church bulletins, graduation programs, and anything else that tells your story. Try to add some notes so people understand what the various items are about or mean to you.

Video cameras are relatively cheap. You can set the camera on a tripod, point it at yourself and talk. Unfortunately, most people find they dry up within a minute or two. It's really useful to have someone ask you questions.

Genealogies are fun. I know a number of folks who have made a retirement career out of researching their family histories. Most communities have a genealogy club you can join.

Bev's brother-in-law Henry phoned her one day and said, "Bring up Google on your computer, type in your maiden name, and see what happens." Bev came up with a genealogy an inch thick when she printed it out.

EDITING OUR MEMORIES

I was delighted, but not a bit surprised, when I read recently of a major study that took place over many years in the eastern United States. A group of folks were interviewed 50 years ago when they were in high school. They were contacted every five years for an update on their lives. The report had some surprising things to say about how they had changed now that they were in their 60s.

The thing that delighted me was that every single one of them had edited their memories. Looking back over the years, especially their teenage years, what they remembered at 65 was not exactly what they had reported when they were 15. And mostly, the memories they had were more pleasant than the reality they reported when they were young.

These people weren't lying. They were simply reflecting part of human nature. So let's not get too hung up on facts. We need to be as accurate as we can, but let's concentrate on the juicy parts of our story – the kinds of people, the meaning of the events, the relationships, and the feelings.

And let's not leave out the spirituality. The traditions of our faith, how our faith was lived and expressed, are a crucial part of the legacy we leave our grandchildren.

It's in this kind of storytelling that our spiritual history unfolds in a natural way. Our real spirituality is not in what we say we believe, but in how we live it now – and how we lived it then. Spirituality is woven right into the warp and woof of the fabric of everyday life.

A few years before she died, I worked with my mother to help her write a short autobiography. Her grandchildren read it eagerly, especially the stories of how their own parents were born.

But Mom left out a most important part of her story. She didn't say anything about the unhappy times

Family faces are magic mirrors. Looking at people who belong to us, we see the past, present and future.

— GAIL LUMET BUCKLEY,
JOURNALIST

in her life. "Well, we don't need to talk about those things," she said when I asked her about it.

But we do. Life is not a waltz through the rose garden. There are tough, painful parts to every life. Our spiritual convictions, if they are to have any value, must be there for us when we encounter pain, sorrow, anger, fear, and disappointment.

Besides, some of the "bad" things are the most fun. I *do* know that my family history includes a relative who sold hair restorer that didn't restore hair, and farm machinery he didn't own. He spent some time in jail. But there's not a word of that in mother's story.

THE LARGER LEGACY

Several years ago I spent a summer in Israel doing biblical studies. It was all very scholarly and dispassionate, but at a more fundamental level it was an exercise in remembering.

Just as I needed to be connected to my mother and who she was, I needed to be connected to my spiritual forebears. I needed to sit with the memory that fills every rock and mountain of that place – to let that memory seep into my bones.

Does it matter? Yes, absolutely. All the ancients from every race and tradition who sat around campfires and told each other stories knew it mattered.

I'm very deeply immersed in my own Christian tradition, which offers me energy and insight and

meaning. But it's no more "true" than any other.

We've had international potluck suppers at our church from time to time. We each try to bring an "ethnic" dish – something out of our cultural heritage. I tend to bring *plūma mouse* (plum soup; "mouse" is pronounced like the small rodent), which comes out of my Russian Mennonite legacy. We all enjoy each other's food and there is never any argument about which is "best" or "most nutritious."

This is important because we live in a multicultural society. Cultural, racial, and religious barriers to marriage are virtually gone. That can result in some bad choices. Some couples decide that rather than choose between one or more cultures, traditions, or faith practices, they won't do any. They settle for a bland McSpirituality. They rob their children of the sense of identity that comes out of family customs and practices – an identity that is essential to the emotional health of children.

It's a bit like saying, "Well, we want our children to make up their own minds about which kind of food they like. We won't make them choose between Mom's cooking and Dad's cooking. We just won't feed them anything."

A PEARL OF GREAT PRICE

Jim and Joan Taylor's daughter, Sharon, has worked hard to discover some of Katherine's Ethiopian ethnicity to bring into their family life. Among other things, Sharon joined a group of other parents who have adopted Ethiopian children. They share ideas and they support each other when troubles emerge.

Joan and Jim have an important role to play in this. They are encouraging Sharon to enrich their own family traditions with traditions from Ethiopia.

It's not our job as grandparents to develop those practices in our grandchildren's home. It is our job to encourage and support our children in this, and to delight in the wealth these spiritual legacies bring us.

I want my grandchildren to know my story. My spirituality is imbedded in that story. I'd be failing my grandchildren – failing to pass on this "pearl of great price" – if I didn't share that with them.

The old are the precious gem in the centre of the household.

~ CHINESE PROVERB

Katherine and her grandpa

7

A Celebration!

id you know there is a "Grandparents' Day"? I didn't, until I started working on this book. It happens each September on the Sunday after Labour Day.

It all began in 1970 when a woman named Marian Lucille Herndon McQuade, in West Virginia, decided we needed a special day to "honour the family and to nurture the love and respect for our elders, our individual heritage, and our unique roots."

It took her eight years until President Jimmy Carter (himself a grandfather) signed the proclamation.

You are the sun, Grandma, you are the sun in my life.
– KITTY TSUI, *AUTHOR*

"The spiritual vocation of the grand-parent is to delight in the grand-child." That key sentence appeared at the beginning of this book. And it seems to me that the appropriate way to celebrate Grandparents' Day is to do some of that delighting.

Let's start with gift giving. It's far more fun giving gifts than receiving them, and the greatest gift we can give to our grandchildren is our-selves. We may shower them with "stuff" and take them to Disneyland, we may hug them and kiss them and send them e-mails and videos, but if we don't give ourselves, we give nothing.

Everyone needs to be needed. When my mother was frail and not able to do many things, she said to me, "The worst thing about being old is that nobody needs you for anything." Children need to be needed too.

It's a two-way street. We need our grandchildren and they need us. They probably can't put words around their need for us. It may even be denied or trivialized. But the need is real nevertheless, and we work to respond to that need and fill our own need as best we can, in whatever circumstances we find ourselves.

Our emotional need is hard to describe and we don't need to. We can simply live it. Often I say to Jake and Zoë, "I need you to sit on my lap for a while." We might phone a grandchild and say, "I've had a tough day and I'm feeling down. Talk to me for a bit about what's happen-ing in your life, and that'll help me feel better." Our mutual need is our gift to each other. Being able to see our own need and the need of our grandchild is the first step toward a healthy relationship. And the first step toward a healthy spirituality.

"Grandparent" isn't a suit we wear. It isn't something we do. It is who we are.

And who we are is our spirituality. None of us know how to define "spiritual grandparenting," but we know it when we experience it.

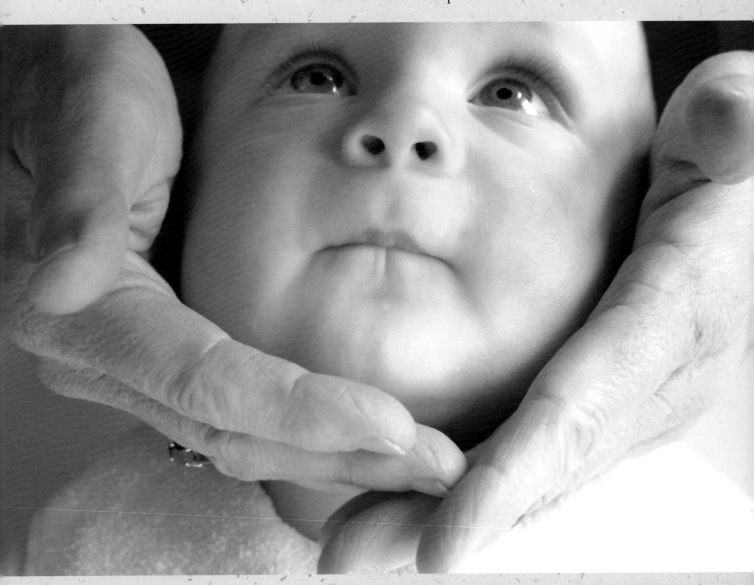

I met her at an Elderhostel. She had a delightfully wrinkled face, and intense blue eyes under a shock of white hair.

My grandfather raised me; my grandmother died before I was born, and my mother suffered terrible bouts of depression. Probably because of my dad, who was an alcoholic. So my grandfather raised me.

Granddad was always so full of life. He read books about all kinds of things – about politics and history and science. He took me to church where they told stories and sang songs. Granddad loved the old Bible stories and he often told me those stories in his own words and his deep blue eyes would sparkle with delight.

And he was involved in politics. He never ran for office or anything, but he cared passionately about the kind of people we elected to office. I remember how upset he would be when our elected leaders did things he thought were wrong.

I was 23 years old when Granddad died. I rushed home from college when my mom phoned to say that Granddad was dying. When I came into the hospital room my mom said, "I think you're too late. Dad is in a coma."

But I talked to him anyway. I thanked him for the care and the love and the stability he gave me. I thanked him for caring passionately about our country and our world. Then, all of a sudden, his eyes flew open. He looked right at me with his deep blue eyes and he smiled and said, "I love you, Elsie. I love you!"

Then he closed his eyes, but the smile stayed on his face until he died a few hours later. I stayed with Mom for a while. She walked around with a kind of vacant look on her face.

About a week later I walked over to the old house where Granddad had lived. It had been sold a few years earlier, when Granddad had to go into a nursing home. In front of the house was the old quince bush he had planted.

As I stood there, a monarch butterfly settled on the bush. Then it flew up and circled me three times before flying off. And I knew that was Granddad. I knew that was Granddad telling me that he was fine and that the love we had for each other wouldn't die.

Elsie is now a grandmother. She had that grandmotherly glow as she showed me snapshots of her two granddaughters. "It was my granddad that showed me how to be a grandmother." She smiled as her hand reached up and touched a brooch she was wearing. It was a simple, pewter brooch – a monarch butterfly.

The voice of an angel

Then there was Margaret. Her son moved in with his girlfriend and before long there was a child. A boy they named Jason.

But then the relationship disintegrated. Margaret's son left the girlfriend who was furious because, among other things, he didn't pick up his share of the childcare costs.

Margaret knew she couldn't do much about the relationship between her son and the girlfriend, but she also knew that she was Jason's grandmother and so she made a decision. "By golly, I decided to *be* a grandmother, no matter what it took," she told me.

It took many phone calls, a lot of patience and a lot of prayer before the girlfriend even allowed Margaret to see her grandchild. But Margaret worked at that relationship, until she was allowed to take Jason on outings, and eventually have Jason stay with her for short and long periods of time. During those times she would read him stories and play games with him. "And at bedtime," she said, "I'd hold him in my arms in the rocker, and I'd rock him to sleep." You can tell by the look in Margaret's eyes that the holding and

the rocking fills her soul as well as Jason's.

Margaret phoned her son and insisted that he come and spend time with his child. That made the girlfriend angry again, but Margaret persisted. "That child needs his father and that father needs his child!"

Margaret often taught Jason songs. "He has the voice of an angel," she said. Jason loved to sing, so Margaret took him to choir practice at her church. He was too young to read the words or the music, but what he didn't pick up at practice Margaret taught him at home. And on Sundays he was there in the front row singing with all the sopranos.

Jason is a teenager now, a big, husky fellow, and his voice is beginning to change. He still comes to visit his grandmother and he still sings in the choir with her every week.

Perfect love sometimes does not come till the first grandchild.

— WELSH PROVERB

Last Sunday in church she was up there doing her work. Her name is Cheryl and she is one of the ministers at the church where Bev and I worship.

And she is very pregnant. I wondered if she would be able to get close enough to the microphone on the pulpit.

That had me woolgathering and wondering what it might be like to bear and birth a child. A nursing friend who worked obstetrics for many years told me men tend to romanticize everything about pregnancy and birth, and that the reality is often quite different.

That's probably true. But as I said, I'm a romantic.

So I remembered a moment in our little RV. We were parked in the driveway at Don and Kari's house, and I had infant Jake in the van with me. He was fussy. Uncomfortable. Crying off and on. And I walked back and forth with him, trying to get him to settle.

Then I remembered hearing that babies find the sound of a beating heart comforting, because that was the sound they heard as they grew in their mother's womb.

So I lay down on the bed and put Jake on his tummy lying on my breast, his head near my heart. I rubbed his back gently and in no time at all he settled down and drifted off to sleep.

I remember thinking, "This is the closest I will ever get to knowing what it is like for a woman to carry a baby in her womb." And I lay there, I don't know how long, in the warm and comforting glow of it.

This, I thought, is the meaning of the word "covenant." Not in the narrow sense of a legal agreement, but in the sense of an unbreakable bond. Jews and Christians both think of themselves as people of the covenant – a bond between the Creator and creation.

I knew then that I will always be Jake's grandfather, and Jake will always be my grandson. There is nothing he can do, nothing I can do, nothing anywhere that can change that.

Grandchildren are the dots that connect the lines from generation to generation.

– LOIS WYSE, *AUTHOR*

Tim Scorer lives on Bowen Island off the west coast of Canada, next door to his grandchildren.

Tim took Emmett, who is eight, on a trip around the island one day, and they stopped at Xenia, a Buddhist retreat centre.

The ground had a fresh covering of snow, and as grandfather and grandson walked the stone-lined labyrinth together theirs were the only footprints visible.

At the centre, they stopped to reflect on the spiral, back-and-forth and around journey that is life. Then Tim said, "Emmett, why don't you pull your cap down over your eyes, and I'll lead you out of the labyrinth."

About a third of the way out, Emmett stopped. "Grandpa," he said, "now you pull your cap down over your eyes, and I'll lead you out of the labyrinth." And so in silence, the child leading the older man, they walked out together.

What did it all mean? Tim used words like "bonding" to describe the experience. But it was more the sense that together they experienced something deeper — something impossible for either of them alone — something transcendent and beautiful.

Perhaps their experience in the labyrinth is a metaphor of life. The grandfather leads the grandchild. Then, over time, the roles reverse and the grandchild leads the grandfather.

A GRANDPARENT GOD

We learn our best lessons from our grandchildren. Zoë and Jake are professors of theology in the school of life where I attend.

I had just been to a religious service – a "Praise Service" it was called – where words like, "we worship you, we adore you, we magnify you, we praise you…" were sung and spoken all evening.

Nothing wrong with that. But it got me thinking. I had been watching our two grandchildren play with their cousins at a family gathering, and realized how grown-up they suddenly were. They didn't pay much attention to the adults. Cousins their age were far more fun to be with. But at one point, on her way by, Zoë looked up and smiled and said, "Hi, Grandpa!" And Jake came by and gave me a friendly little pummelling with his fists. Just for a few seconds, then he was off again.

In many faith traditions, the metaphor for God is often grandfather or grandmother. I like that. And my experience as a grandfather has me wondering what God would want from grandchildren. From us.

Does our Creator really want our praise? Does God really want to be thanked?

I've never wanted praise and flattery from my grandchildren. But when they climb on my knee and tell me about school, about their friends, or show me a book they have enjoyed, that is what I need and want. It's the relationship I crave.

When they are ill or unhappy, they will come and sit with us. Just

My son, you ought to be of some help to your fellow men… Our grandfather who stands in our midst sends forth all kinds of blessings. Try then to obtain one of these. Then, some day as you travel along the road of life, you will know what to do and encounter no obstacles.

– WINNEBEGO FATHER'S PRECEPTS

quietly. There's nothing to be done or said, but being close to a loved one helps.

When we give Zoë or Jake gifts, Kari makes sure they say thanks, but what I look for is the sparkle of delight in their eyes.

Should we say thanks to our Creator for all of creation's gifts, including the gift of grandchildren? Sure. But I wonder if what a grandparent God really yearns for is the shining delight in our eyes. God simply yearns for us to live our delight.

If we find deep spiritual joy and comfort in our Creator's gifts, we will want to take care of them and participate in the divine process of a continuing creation.

All that thanksgiving rhetoric and praise must get pretty tiresome to God, especially if we do not delight in creation. Especially if we don't *live* it.

Our grandchildren will notice that too – if our words of praise and thanksgiving don't translate into respect and care for God's creation. If the words we say and the words we live don't match, they will know.

There's a little ritual we go through after each visit with our grandchildren. Bev and I get into the car. Zoë and Jake run to the front window of the house (or to the front gate if it's nice out), and wave as we come by. We slow down, wave back, and give the horn a toot.

Do you suppose our services of worship might be something like that? Do you suppose a grandparent God looks for that kind of simple, delightful response from us?

A FINAL GIFT

It was noon on the Saturday between Good Friday and Easter. I stood in a cemetery with my family and my extended family – the family we joined through the marriage of our daughter Kari to Don.

We were there to bury the ashes of Margaret, who was mother, grandmother, aunt, and dear friend to the people in that circle.

I've been to a number of committal services. They consisted usually of a prayer, maybe a short homily, a bit of scripture, and perhaps putting handfuls of soil into the grave. Most families want nothing more than that.

But in this service the grandchildren wrote messages to Grandma on a small banner, and then her children knelt around the tiny grave and carefully placed the small casket of ashes in a larger casket, along with the banner, some family photos, a chocolate candy, and a favourite shawl she often wore.

And there were tears. Good, healthy tears.

There was no primitive theology involved in all this. There was no talk of things she would "need for her journey." Margaret's children were simply acting out their love. Words are too slippery for times like this. And so they used the language of symbols.

When the attendant brought the wheelbarrow of soil to fill in the

Give selflessly to your grandchildren from the bountiful harvest of your ripened soul. In doing so, you will touch the future. That is the only way to be ready to leave this life when your time comes.

– ARTHUR KORNHABER,
AUTHOR

We say goodbye to Grandma Margaret

155

grave, he handed the shovel to us, and again all of us, even the youngest, had a part in closing the grave.

The attendant finished and left, but we stayed on, talking, looking at gravestones. The cemetery seemed a place of life, even though the clouds rolled overhead and the wind was cold.

I discovered the headstone of a friend, Clyde Woollard, who died a few years ago, and I smiled at the memory of how he had made a hole-in-one in golf just a few weeks before he died. And how he laughed at himself a week later when he shot an eight on the same hole.

Zoë and the other children also looked at gravestones. "Grandma," she said, talking Bev's hand, "there's a gravestone here for a baby who only lived for one day." The two stood quietly together for a few bright moments gazing at the stone. Then Zoë bounced off to join her cousins.

Grandma Margaret's dying, and the death of Grandpa Frank a few years earlier, were family affairs. The children were not protected from death's reality nor shielded from its mysteries. They were not herded away and fed euphemisms to hide reality. Even as their grandparents faded slowly into death, they visited regularly, as they had done all their lives.

Grandma Margaret and Grandpa Frank left a gift. Don's words are worth repeating. "You are never too old to be loved. You are never too sick to be loved. You may be forgetful and strange, you may be old and frail, but the love is still there."

Having not been protected from the pain of death, the grandchildren were able to sense some of the beauty of death – the hope of death – the holy mystery of death.

When the white wings of death take us on our final journey, perhaps the last and best gift we as grandparents can give to our grandchildren is this.

How to love.

How to live.

And, in the fullness of time, how to let go of this life.

Resources

A wide variety of resources are available to grandparents. If you Google "grandparenting" or "grandparents" on the web, you'll find a wide variety of websites and links that can be informative and often fun.

But please be careful. Many people on the web simply want to sell you something. Some of them are not very responsible. Some are out to fleece you. It's best to stay with known organizations, and the links they provide through their web pages.

Many communities publish lists of agencies and organizations of interest to grandparents and for retired people. Some communities have a helpline to which you can take your situation, and where you can locate the appropriate contacts or assistance.

Magazines and Websites

CARP: The Canadian Association of Retired People
website: www.carp.ca
e-mail: carp@50plus.com
Suite 1304, 27 Queen St. E.,
Toronto, ON, Canada, M5C 2M6
1-800-363-9736

AARP: The American Association of Retired People
website www.aarp.org
601 E Street NW
Washington, DC, 20049, USA
1-888-687-2277

Grandparents Magazine
website: www.grandparentsmagazine.net
281 Rosedale Ave.
Wayne, PA, 19087, USA

CANGRADS – information and support for Canadian grandparents
website: www.cangrands.com
e-mail: grandma@cangrands.com
RR 1, McArthurs Mills, ON,
K0L 2M0, Canada

GrandParents' Web
website: www.cyberparent.com/gran
no postal address available

Books

Bengston, V. L. and J. F. Robertson, eds. *Grandparenthood*. Beverley Hills: Safe, 1985.

Bliezner, R. and V.H. Bedford. *Handbook of Aging and the Family*. Westport, CT: Greenwood, 1995.

Bly, Stephen and Jane. *The Power of a Godly Grandparent: Leaving a Spiritual Legacy*. Kansas City, MO: Beacon Hill Publishing, 2003. This is a helpful book, written from a conservative Christian perspective.

Kornhaber, Arthur, M.D. *Contemporary Grandparenting*. Thousand Oaks, CA: Sage Publications, 2005.
— *The Grandparent Solution*. San Francisco: Jossey-Bass, 2004.
— *The Grandparent Guide*. Whitby, ON: McGraw-Hill, 2002.
— *Grandparent Power!* New York: Three Rivers Press, 1995.
— *Grandparents, Grandchildren: the Vital Connection*. New York: Anchor Books, 1981. Kornhaber is easily the most widely known authority on grandparenting.

L'Engle, Madeleine. *The Summer of the Great-Grandmother.* San Francisco: Harper & Row, Publishers, 1974. This book is now out of print, but it is a delightful, moving and perceptive account of the last days of L'Engle's mother. Worth chasing down through used book stores.

Sonnheim, Moshe, D.S.W. *Welcome to the Club: The Art of Jewish Grandparenting.* Jerusalem-New York: Devora Publishing, 2004.

Szinovacz, M. E. *Handbook on Grandparenthood.* Westport, CT: Greenwood, 1998.

Wassermann, Selma. *The Long Distance Grandmother: How to Stay Close to Distant Grandchildren.* Point Roberts, WA, and Vancouver, BC: Hartley & Marks, 1990. This book is out of print, and somewhat out of date. But it still has many useful ideas for long-distance grandparents. Worth chasing down through used book stores.

Weaver, Andrew J. and Carolyn L. Stapleton, eds. *Wells of Wisdom: Grandparents and Spiritual Journeys.* Cleveland: The Pilgrim Press, 2005. A series of grandparenting reflections by a distinguished group of Catholic and Protestant writers.

OTHER NORTHSTONE BOOKS

Visit www.woodlakebooks.com or your nearest bookseller.

Hickling, Meg. *The New Speaking of Sex.* Kelowna, BC: Northstone, 2005. An exceptionally useful book for both parents and grandparents. This is not a how-babies-are-made kind of book, but about the conversations we have with children. Children learn a great deal about sex from their friends, but much of it is false and potentially hurtful. Sometimes grandparents find themselves in a unique position to talk about sexuality with their grandchildren in a way that the parents can't. Or won't. These books will help you be ready.

Milton, Ralph. *The Family Story Bible.* Kelowna, BC: Northstone, 1996 (Canada), Westminster/John Knox (USA). Thousands of grandparents have purchased this book as a gift for their grandchildren. It retells favourite Bible stories in contemporary language and reflects an inclusive and grace-filled theology.

For those who would like to take this a step further, a much-expanded version is available in the *Lectionary Story Bible*. This is a three-volume set, one book for each year of the *Revised Common Lectionary* cycle, with at least one and usually two (sometimes three) stories based on the lectionary readings for each Sunday.

OTHER *SPIRITUALITY OF…* BOOKS

The Spirituality of Wine by Tom Harpur (Northstone, 2004)
The Spirituality of Mazes & Labyrinths by Gailand MacQueen (Northstone, 2005)
The Spirituality of Gardening by Donna Sinclair (Northstone, 2005)
The Spirituality of Art by Lois Huey-Heck and Jim Kalnin (Northstone, 2006)
The Spirituality of Pets by James Taylor (Northstone, 2006)
The Spirituality of Bread by Donna Sinclair (Northstone, 2007)

All of these beautifully illustrated and written books can help you find the spirituality in the ordinary things of life. As we deepen our own spirituality, we will be able to live it in the presence of our grandchildren.
Visit www.woodlakebooks.com or your nearest bookseller.

Other Resources

Educational and Retreat Centres
A wide variety of retreat and continuing educational events are offered by denominations, religious groups, and educational institutions. Some of them are intergenerational events for grandparents and grandchildren, often in a summer vacation-style location. Check with such organizations through the various institutions and places of worship. Double-check possibilities you may find on the web, because they may offer more than they can deliver. Find somebody who is "in-the-know."

Elderhostel is an American-based, non-profit organization that provides educational study and travel opportunities at reasonable cost for seniors. Not only are their programs interesting, but the seniors who attend tend to be lively and interesting. Each year, Elderhostel also offers intergenerational events specifically so grandparents and grandchildren can enjoy study and travel together.

Website: www.elderhostel.org
Elderhostel
13 Avenue de Lafayette,
Boston, MA, 02111, USA
1-800-454-5768.